Classic Acting Monologues for Boys

(aged 8 -14yrs)

Compiled & edited by Kim Gilbert

Copyright © 2020 Kim Gilbert
All rights reserved.
ISBN: 9798573791036

DEDICATION

This collection of acting monologues is dedicated to all teachers and students of drama with a love of performing from the classics. There is something for every young performer to choose from. All of the characters in this book have been chosen carefully and are most suited to the 8-14 yr age range. These scenes are suitable for a wide range of study, performance, exams and festivals.

ACKNOWLEDGEMENTS

A special thanks goes to my husband Steve, who has prepared this collection for publication, and has bailed me out on numerous occasions over the years, with his technical expertise.

TABLE OF CONTENTS

Introduction	1
Acting a role	2
Acting Style	4
<u>Peter Pan</u>	8
Hook	10
<u>The Wizard of Oz</u>	
Professor Marvel	11
Scarecrow	13
Tin Man	15
Wizard	16
<u>Alice in Wonderland</u>	
The Cheshire Cat	19
Caterpillar	20
<u>The Pied Piper of Hamelin:</u>	
<u>Piper</u>	21
<u>Aladdin</u>	
The Pedlar	22
<u>Hansel & Gretel</u>	
Hansel	23

The Princess & the Swineherd

Emperor   25

King Midas   26

The Lion, the Witch & the Wardrobe

Mr Tumnus   28

Edmund   30

Mr Beaver   31

The Voyage of the Dawn Treader

Eustace   33

Great Expectations

Pip   35

Hard Times

Tom Gradgrind   36

Oliver

Dodger   37

A Christmas Carol

Nephew   40

The Secret Garden

Dickon   41

Colin   43

The Snow Queen

Storyteller   47

Puss in Boots

Miller's Son   49

The Tinder Box

White Dog   50

Worzel Gummidge   51

Toad of Toad Hall

Rat   52

Mole   54

Toad   56

Badger   57

Toad   59

Chief Weasel   61

The House at Pooh Corner

Eeyore   63

Tom Sawyer   65

Pinocchio

Gepetto   66

Pinocchio   68

The Happy Prince

Prince71

The Remarkable Rocket

Rocket73

Androcles & the Lion

Androcles77

Heidi

Peter81

A Midsummer Night's Dream

Puck83

Henry V

Boy85

King John

Prince Arthur86

The Merchant of Venice

Launcelot Gobbo87

Twelfth Night

Sebastian88

The Murder in the Red Barn

William Corder											89

The Railway Children

Peter												91

## The Snowman												92

Jane Eyre

John Reed											94

The Little Mermaid

Prince												95

## Noah												96

The Silver Chair

Golg												98

Eustace												99

## The Horse & his boy										101

Author index											102

About the Author										103

INTRODUCTION

I have compiled and edited this collection of classic monologues for young boys to study, perform and enjoy. These scenes are suitable for a range of acting exams and awards as well as for auditions and festivals. I have tried and tested these scenes with numerous students over the years with great success and more importantly, they have thoroughly enjoyed working on them. I believe, it is crucial to choose characters within ones' playing range. This collection contains a range of characters suited to be played by young boys from the age of approximately 8yrs to 14 yrs. From my experience, I have seen many young actors tackling characters which are often unsuited to their age range and skills. There will be plenty of time in the future to tackle the more mature and demanding male characters which are available to play from a wealth of drama and literature. Learn to build your skills and technique slowly and systematically with the younger, and age-appropriate characters before you attempt to move forwards to the demands of older and more complex characters.

The monologues in this collection are taken from a range of plays and classic novels: Peter Pan, The Secret Garden, The Wizard of Oz, Tom Sawyer, The Wind in the Willows, The Narnia Chronicles, Shakespeare, Dickens novels and many more. Each scene has an introduction prepared suitable for exam or festival work and are also timed with exams and festival work in mind. I hope you enjoy this collection.

ACTING A ROLE

When preparing for acting a role one should always study the play as a whole if possible and approach your chosen scene in context within the whole play.

Here are some questions to consider:

Is your character a central character or leading character?

Is your character crucial to the development of the plot?

Is your character a stock character or small cameo role, providing a sub-plot, comedy or light relief to the plot?

What does your character look like in terms of physical appearance? This can be considered in terms of age, height, weight, physique, posture, colouring etc.

How do you envisage your character in costume? Do you need to consider the historical period for your chosen role and research the type of costume you would be wearing?

Think about how you might like to play your character in terms of physical and vocal skills? Is your natural voice appropriate or do you need to characterise your voice and speak with an accent or dialect?

How does your character develop throughout the play?

Try to map your character's journey throughout the play?

What are your character's likes, dislikes?

How do you relate to your character and how does your character relate to the other characters in the play?

What do you like about your character? Try to create a backstory for your character.

What is your character's role/purpose in the play? Try to establish his objective within the scene you are playing or even in the play as a whole (super-objective).

Consider casting. Is this role a good choice for you? Does this character suit your acting skills and personality?

What skills and characteristics do you need as an actor to play this character?

ACTING STYLE

It is important to adopt the correct style of acting for your chosen performance piece. You will need to consider whether your scene is perhaps from the realist school of writing, or whether you are performing Shakespeare and need to acquire knowledge of the metre which Shakespeare writes in. Or perhaps you have chosen a piece which relies purely on fantasy and imagination. These are all choices you will have to consider when tackling a scene.

Fantasy

This style of acting has no limitations. In fantasy, anything can happen and the actor has great scope to use their imagination. This style is not to be taken too seriously and offers the young actor great creativity. Many children's plays involve fantasy and are popular choices with young players. These plays are a good starting point for young actors. The style of acting is often larger than life and 'overacting' in these types of roles is common and acceptable.

Comedy and Tragedy

It is necessary to identify the genre of your play as this will affect your playing style. Good timing is essential in comedy and many roles will require a heightened use of realism to create the desired comic effect. However, if you are playing tragedy, a more serious and sombre acting style will be required. There are many styles of acting and these need to be identified and an appropriate playing style adopted, according to the writing style of your chosen play.

Acting Shakespeare

Shakespeare's characters are depicted as real people with 'universal' emotions even though they generally speak in verse. His variety of characters interrelate with other characters creating great interest within the plot. Apart from his leading characters, his comedies often include stock-characters, which are easily recognizable characters with common features and characteristics.

Iambic Pentametre

This is the metre used by Shakespeare and many other writers and is made up of 5 feet of iambic rhythms.e.g. de dum/de dum/de dum/de dum/de dum. e.g. 'The clock struck nine when I did send the nurse' (Romeo & Juliet) and 'I left no ring with her, what means this lady?' (Twelfth Night).

The rhythm of iambic pentameter resembles the beating of the human heart and is closest to the natural rhythms of everyday speech.

Blank Verse

Blank verse is verse without rhyme and is suited to play writing as it sounds more natural.

Realism

Realism, is a literary technique which describes locations, characters and themes in a realistic style without using elaborate imagery or rhetorical language. This means that the emotions of the characters have to be sincere and believable.

Playing the Objective

The Theatre Practitioner, Constantine Stanislavski, suggested that a whole play be separated into a series of smaller scenes or units of performance. In each unit there will be an objective. The objectives from these units will form or lead to a Super objective.

Basically, playing the objective means identifying what your character is trying to achieve in each scene? What is your character's motivation? If this goal can be established, the performer will have discovered an overall objective.

When analyzing a play, you should look for its' overall aim or theme. The scenes can be broken up into parts. Decide on the objective for each scene or unit. Ideally, the objective should be considered as a verb, an action; something your character ideally wants to do or achieve.

Period

You should be aware of the period of the writing style and consider the manners which were used during this time. This also means considering the costumes worn during the period.

Truth

The actor should always aim to perform with truth, imagination and sincerity. Spontaneity in acting is key in order to convince your audience and be credible.

THE MONOLOGUES

PETER PAN
BY J M BARRIE

(Peter Pan can easily be played by a boy or girl. In this scene, Peter has entered the Darling's house through an open window. Peter meets Wendy for the first time).

Peter:

Wendy, don't withdraw. I can't help crowing, when I'm pleased with myself. Wendy – One girl is worth more than twenty boys.

I ran away the day I was born because I heard Father and Mother talking of what I was to be when I became a man. I want always to be a little boy and to have fun; so, I ran away to Kensington Gardens and lived a long time among the fairies. But they are nearly all dead now. You see, Wendy, when the first baby laughed for the first time, the laugh broke into a thousand pieces and they all went skipping about, and that was the beginning of fairies. And now, when every new baby is born, it's first laugh becomes a fairy. So, there *ought* to be one fairy for every boy or girl. But there isn't. Children know such a lot now. Soon they won't believe in fairies, and every time a child says "I don't believe in fairies," there is a fairy somewhere that falls down dead.
(Peter calls out to his fairy).
Tinker Bell, Tink, where are you?

You don't hear anything, do you? A tinkle of bells. That's the fairy language.

Wendy, I believe I shut her up in that drawer! Oh, she's behind the clock.

Tink, this lady wishes you were her fairy.

She is not very polite. She says you are a great ugly girl, and that she is *my* fairy.
You know, Tink, you can't be my fairy because I am a gentleman and you are a lady.

She is called Tinker Bell because she mends the fairy pots and kettles. She lives with the Lost Boys. They are the children who fall out of their prams when the nurse is looking the other way. If they are not claimed within seven days, they are sent far away to Never Land. I'm Captain. But we are rather lonely. You see, Wendy, we have no female companionship.

Come on, Wendy! Let's fly! I'll teach you. I'll teach you how to jump on the wind's back and then away we go. You just think wonderful thoughts and they lift you up in the air. I must blow fairy dust on you first. Just wriggle your shoulders this way, and then let go!

PETER PAN
BY J.M BARRIE

(The evil Captain Hook is on his pirate ship. He is leaning against the mast and prowling the deck).

Hook:

How still the night is; nothing sounds alive. Now is the hour when children in their homes are a-bed; their lips bright-browned with the good-night chocolate, and their tongues drowsily searching for belated crumbs housed insecurely on their shining cheeks. Compare with them the children on this boat about to walk the plank. Split my infinitives, but 'tis my hour of triumph! (*He dances a few jubilant steps).* And yet some disky spirit compels me now to make my dying speech, lest when dying there may be no time for it. All mortals envy me, yet better perhaps for Hook to have had less ambition! O fame, fame, thou glittering bauble!

No little children love me. I am told they play at Peter Pan, and that the strongest always chooses to be Peter. They would rather be a Twin than Captain Hook; they force the baby to be Hook. The baby! That is where the canker gnaws. 'Tis said they find Smee lovable. But an hour ago I found him letting the youngest of them try on his spectacles. Pathetic Smee, the Nonconformist pirate, a happy smile up on his face because he thinks they fear him! How can I break it to him that they think him lovable? No, bi-carbonate of soda, no, not even!

Quiet, you dog, or I'll cast anchor on you!

Are all the prisoners chained, so that they can't fly away?

Get the plank ready!

THE WIZARD OF OZ
BY L FRANK BAUM

(Dorothy meets Professor Marvel. Professor Marvel purports to be able to see into the future. However, he is what is called a 'quack').

Professor Marvel:

Well – well – well! Houseguests, huh? (*Laughing*) Ha, ha, ha, ha! And who might you be? Heh! (*To Dorothy*).
No, no, no, now don't tell me!
Let's see … you're … you're traveling in disguise – No, that's not right … I … you're … you're going on a visit – No! I'm wrong … that's … you're … you're … running away!

Ha, ha! Professor Marvel never guesses – he knows! Now why are you running away?

No, no, now don't tell me. They … they don't understand you at home. They don't appreciate you … you want to see other lands – big cities – big mountains – big oceans … heh!

You want to come with me and see all the crowned heads of Europe? Well, I … never do anything without consulting my crystal first. Let's go inside here. We'll … just come along. I'll show you …

(Dorothy and the Professor enter his wagon where there are all sorts of fortune telling gadgets).
Here, sit right down here, that's it! Heh, heh! This … this is the same, genuine, magic, authentic crystal used by the priests of Isis and Osiris in the days of the Pharaohs of Egypt … in which Cleopatra first saw the approach of Julius Caesar and Marc Antony … and … and so on and so on. Now, you, ah … you'd better close your eyes, my child, for a moment … in order to be better in tune with the infinite … we … we can't do these things without reaching

out into the infinite ...
(Whilst Dorothy has her eyes closed, the Professor searches through her basket and finds a photograph of the farm and Auntie Em).

Now you can open your eyes. We'll gaze into the crystal! Ah, what's this I see? A house ... with a picket fence and a barn with a weather vane and ... of a ... of a ... running horse. Yes ... there's ... there's a woman ... she's ... she's wearing a ... polka-dot dress ... her face is care-worn ... Yes, her ... her name is Emily. I can't quite see ... Why – she's crying! Someone has hurt her ... someone has just about broken her heart ... It's someone she loves very much. Someone she's been very kind to. Someone she's taken care of in sickness. (He is *gazing into his crystal ball)*. Why, she's putting her hand on her heart! Why, she's dropping down on the bed!

Eh, that's all. The crystal's gone dark.

(Dorothy panics and runs off).

But what's this? I thought you were going along with me? There's a storm blowin' up – Poor little kid! I hope she gets home all right.

THE WIZARD OF OZ
BY L. FRANK BAUM

(The scarecrow meets Dorothy Gale and asks her if he can go with her, in search of the great wizard in order to grant him some brains).

Scarecrow:

It's pleasant down that way too! (*pointing to the left*). Of course, people do go that way, too! (*pointing in both directions*). That's the trouble, I can't make up my mind. I haven't got a brain – only straw. I don't know how I can talk but some people without brains do an awful lot of talking, don't they?

How do you do?

It's very tedious being stuck up here all day long with a pole up your back. I can't get down.

Oh, that's very kind of you – very kind. I'm not bright about doing things, but if you'll just bend the nail down in the back, maybe I'll slip off and come *(Dorothy does what he asks).* – Ohhhh! Whoops! There goes some of me again! My! It's good to be free!

Did I scare you? (*Sadly*). I didn't think so.

(A crow lights on his shoulder at this moment). Boo! Scat! Boo! You see, I can't even scare a crow! They come from miles around just to eat in my field and … and laugh in my face. Oh, I'm a failure, because I haven't got a brain!

(Dorothy tells him that she is going to see a wizard).

You're going to see a wizard? Do you think if I went with you, this Wizard would give me some brains?

Witch? Hmmm! I'm not afraid of a witch. I'm not afraid of anything – *(He whispers).* Oh, except a lighted match. *(He touches his straw).* But I'd face a whole box full of them for the chance of getting some brains. (*Pleading*). Look, I won't be any trouble, because I don't eat a thing; and I won't try to manage things, because I can't think. Uh … won't you take me with you?

(Dorothy agrees to take him with her to see the Wizard).

Hooray! We're off to see a wizard! To Oz!

THE WIZARD OF OZ
BY L FRANK BAUM

(Dorothy meets the Tin Man. He can't move because he needs oiling. They invite him to the Emerald City to visit Oz to ask him for a heart).

<u>Tin Man:</u>

Oil can! Oil can! Oil can!

(Dorothy finds some oil and loosens the tin man's mouth).

My mouth … my mouth!

M-m-my, my, my, my, my goodness! I can talk again! Oh, oil my arms, please! Oil my elbows! Oh!

(Dorothy & the scarecrow oil the tin man's various joints).

No, I'm fine. It feels wonderful! I've held that axe up for ages. Oh!

I've been like this since about a year ago. I was chopping a tree, when suddenly it began to rain. And right in the middle of a chop, I rusted solid. I've been that way ever since.

Oh, my neck! Bang on my chest if you think I'm perfect. Go ahead – bang on it! *(The scarecrow bangs on his chest).* It's empty. The tinsmith forgot to give me a heart. No heart! All hollow!

Could I come with you to the Emerald City to ask the Wizard of Oz for a heart?

THE WIZARD OF OZ
BY L FRANK BAUM

(The Wizard in this story is found out to be a fraud. He is not great and powerful as he made Dorothy, the Scarecrow, Tin Man and Lion believe. He is a mere mortal and now that he has been found out, he gives them some very useful advice).

Wizard:

I'm afraid it's true. There's no other Wizard except me. I'm a humbug. I'm a very good man – I'm just a very bad wizard.

Anybody can have a brain. That's a very mediocre commodity. Every pusillanimous creature that crawls on the earth or slinks through slimy seas has a brain! Back where I come from, we have universities, seats of great learning – where men go to become great thinkers – and when they come out, they think deep thoughts – and with no more brains than you have – But! They have one thing you haven't got! A diploma.

(The Wizard presents Scarecrow with a diploma on parchment paper).

Therefore – by virtue of the authority vested in me by the Universitatus Committeeatum e pluribus unum, I hereby confer upon you the honorary degree of Th. D. Heh, heh! Th. D – that's the Doctor of Thinkology.

(To the lion) As for you, my fine friend, you're a victim of disorganized thinking. You are under the unfortunate delusion that simply because you run away from danger, you have no courage. You're confusing courage with wisdom. Back where I come from, we have men who are called heroes. Once a

year they take their fortitude out of mothballs and parade it down the main street of the city. And they have no more courage than you have – But! They have one thing that you haven't got! A medal!

(He takes out a big medal and pins it on the Lion's chest).

Therefore, for meritorious conduct, extraordinary valour, conspicuous bravery against wicked witches, I award you the Triple Cross. You are now a member of the Legion of Courage. *(He kisses Lion on both cheeks).*

As for you, my galvanised friend, you want a heart! You don't know how lucky you are not to have one. Hearts will never be practical until they can be made unbreakable. Back where I come from, there are men who do nothing all day but good deeds. They are called phil … er … phil … er …yes … good-deed-doers, and their hearts are no bigger than yours – But! They have one thing you haven't got! A testimonial!

(He takes a huge heart-shaped watch and chain out of his bag and gives it to the Tin Man).
Therefore, in consideration of your kindness, I take pleasure at this time in presenting you with a small token of our esteem and affection. And remember, my sentimental friend, that a heart is not judged by how much you love, but by how much you are loved by others.

(To Dorothy).

Well, you Dorothy, force me into a cataclysmic decision. The only way to get Dorothy back to Kansas is for me to take her there myself. I'm an old Kansas man myself … born and bred in the heart of the western wilderness, premier balloonist par excellence to the Miracle Wonderland Carnival Company –

until one day, while performing spectacular feats of stratospheric skill never before attempted by civilized man, an unfortunate phenomenon occurred. The balloon failed to return to the fair. Frightened! You are talking to a man who has laughed in the face of death, sneered at doom, and chuckled at catastrophe. I was petrified! Then suddenly the wind changed, and the balloon floated down in to the heart of this noble city, where I was instantly acclaimed Oz, the First Wizard deluxe! *(He laughs).* Times being what they were, I accepted the job, retaining my balloon against the advent of a quick getaway. Ha, Ha! And in that balloon, my dear Dorothy, you and I will return to the land of *e pluribus unum*!

(The Wizard takes Dorothy to a large balloon which is erected on a decorated platform).

My friends, my friends ... This is positively the finest exhibition ever to be shown ... well... eh ... well ... be that as it may – I, your Wizard, am about to embark upon a hazardous and technically unexplainable journey into the outer stratosphere... to confer, converse, and otherwise hobnob with my brother wizards, and I hereby decree that until what time – if any – that I return, the Scarecrow by virtue of his highly superior brains, shall rule in my stead, assisted by the Tin Man, by virtue of his magnificent heart, and the Lion, by virtue of his courage! Obey them as you would me! Thankyou!

ALICE IN WONDERLAND
BY LEWIS CARROLL

(The Cheshire tree is sitting on a bough of a tree, grinning. It has very long claws and a great many teeth. The cat addresses Alice).

The Cheshire Cat:

Gracious me, there is that girl, Alice, again. The one who took the Duchess's baby.

Good day, can I help you? Which way to walk? Well, that depends a good deal on where you want to get to. If you don't care about where, it doesn't matter which way you go – you're bound to get somewhere if you only walk long enough.

In that direction, lives a Hatter; and in that direction, lives a March hare. Visit either you like; they're both mad. You can't help going amongst mad people here. We're all mad. I'm mad. You're mad. You must be mad or you wouldn't have come here. How do I know that you're mad? To begin with, a dog's not mad. You grant that? Well, then, you see a dog growls when it's angry, and wags its tail when it's pleased. Now I growl when I'm pleased, and wag my tail when I'm angry. Therefore, I'm mad. Purring, or growling, call it what you like. Do you play croquet with the Queen today? Well, you haven't been invited yet? But, you'll see me there.

(The cat vanishes for a while then re-appears).

By the bye, what became of the baby? I'd nearly forgotten to ask. Turned into a pig? I thought it would. Did you say pig or fig? I'm sorry if I'm making you giddy appearing and vanishing so suddenly; I didn't mean to make you giddy!

(The Cheshire cat disappears slowly, leaving only his grin).

ALICE IN WONDERLAND
BY LEWIS CARROLL

(A caterpillar, smoking a hookah, confronts Alice. He is sitting on a rather large mushroom).

The Caterpillar:

Who are you? What do you mean by – I hardly know! Explain yourself! Not yourself? – no, I don't see! Turn into a chrysalis – someday, and then a butterfly! No, that's not a bit queer! Who are you?

(Alice walks away).

Come back, I've something important to say. *(Alice comes back).* Keep your temper! So, you think you're changed, do you? How? You can't remember what things? Repeat 'You are old, Father William'. *(He listens to Alice trying to recite the poem).* That is not said right, it is wrong from beginning to end.

What size do you want to be? Are you content now? A little larger? Three inches is a very good height indeed! You'll get used to it in time.

(He begins smoking his hookah again. He climbs down from his mushroom).

One side of this mushroom will make you grow taller, and the other side will make you grow shorter. You'll have to find out which is which!

(He slithers away and disappears from sight).

THE PIED PIPER OF HAMELIN
BY ROBERT BROWNING

(The Pied Piper is speaking to the Mayor of Hamelin. The city has been plagued by rats and the Piper has a solution to get rid of them. This extract comes from the famous poem by Robert Browning).

<u>Pied Piper:</u>

Please your honours, I am able,
By means of a secret charm, to draw
All creatures living beneath the sun,
That creep, or swim, or fly, or run,
After me so as you never saw!
And I chiefly use my charm
On creatures that do people harm,
The mole and toad and newt and viper;
And people call me the Pied Piper.
You will notice round my neck
A scarf of red and yellow stripe,
To match with my coat of the self-same check;
And at the scarf's end, hangs my pipe.
My fingers, are forever straying
In impatience to be playing
Upon my pipe, as low it dangle
Over my vesture so sold-fangled.
Yet I, poor piper as I am,
In Tartary freed the Cham
Last June, from a huge swarm of gnats;
I eased in Asia the Nizam
Of a monstrous brook of vampire-bats:
And as for what your brain bewilders,
If I can rid your town of rats
Will you give me a thousand guilders?

ALADDIN
BY ANTOINE GALLAND (1712)

(Aladdin is a folk tale originating from the Middle East. Aladdin is visiting a street market when a pedlar tries to sell him an old lamp).

The Pedlar:

Ah, Salaam and good evening to you, worthy friend. Please, please, come closer.

That's too close, a little too close.

There, Welcome to Agrabah. City of mystery, of enchantment, and the finest merchandise this side of the river Jordan, on sale today, come on down!

Heh, hey. Look at this! Yes! It will not break – will not –oh, it broke. Ohhhhhh!

Look at this!

I have never seen one of these intact before. This is from the famous Dead Sea. Listen. It's very good. Wait, don't go!

I can see that you're only interested in the exceptionally rare. I think then, you would be most rewarded to consider... this! *(He shows Aladdin the lamp).* Do not be fooled by its commonplace appearance. Like so many things, it is not what is outside, but what is inside that counts. This is no ordinary lamp! It once changed the course of a young man's life. A young man that liked this lamp was more than what he seemed.

Perhaps you would like to hear the tale?
It begins on a dark night …

HANSEL & GRETEL
BY THE GRIMM BROTHERS.

(Hansel and his sister, Gretel, have been left in the forest by their father. Their wicked stepmother has insisted he leave them there. They try to return home on two occasions but keep getting lost. They come across a house of candy which is owned by a wicked witch whose aim is to fatten them up and eat them).

Hansel:

Don't cry, Gretel. Please don't cry. We'll find a way to get out of the forest. Just wait awhile until the moon has risen. Then we'll find the way home. Father didn't mean to leave us all alone in the forest. I've broken up the bread and left a trail of breadcrumbs to lead us back home again. We should be able to easily find our way back home again. Just wait until the moon has risen, Gretel. Then we'll see the little breadcrumbs that I scattered. They'll show us the way back home. Let's see! Here is a breadcrumb – and here – oh no! The trail has stopped! The birds must have eaten the breadcrumbs up and there's hardly anything left.

Look, over there! A house! I wonder if there is anyone in? Let's see! Why, it's covered in gingerbread! It has cake for a roof and pure sugar for windows. What a blessed meal! Let's have a taste. I want to eat a piece of the roof. Gretel, you can have some of the window, since it's so sweet.

(A shrill voice from a witch cries out from inside the house. It is very frightening for them).

What was that? No, there's no one here. It's only the wind, the wind; it's very mild, blowing like the Heavenly Child. There's no one here!

(The witch enters and lures them into her house).

Oh! We're so very sorry. We haven't eaten for days and we're so hungry. Will you give us something to eat?

Milk and pancakes with sugar and apples and nuts? How wonderful!

THE PRINCESS & THE SWINEHERD
BY HANS CHRISTIAN ANDERSON (1841)

(The Emperor speaks to Dominic who is pretending to be a servant. Dominic is interested in the Emperor's daughter, the princess).

Emperor:

What is your name? You wanted to speak to me. Then, come out of your daydream, and do so. I asked your name. There's no need to spell it. Oliver? As good as any. And you want work in my gardens? For any particular reason? You like gardening – do you, indeed? Will you show me your hands? (*The Emperor notices that Dominic is wearing a diamond ring).* Yes, you're accustomed to use them. They would be gentle with plants … and animals. Hm! Yes, I think I see. Now, what shall I do with you? I've a full complement in the gardening line, I'm afraid. Ah, what will you say to this, I wonder? Do you see that little hut down there, by the stream? Would you live in that, and look after my pigs? They might be very interesting, when you get used to them. Then find my head gardener, in the Mews, and he will help you to settle in as the new swineherd. The pigs have been rather neglected lately. Their last man suddenly had a brainstorm and joined the Army. You know how it is; when no one quite knows how to handle things, they get temperamental. But I'm nearly sure you'll find a way to deal with everything. Good afternoon, and I trust you'll be a great success … as a swineherd, of course.

KING MIDAS - A LEGEND.

(This story is from a Greek legend. King Midas was a greedy and foolish man whose only interest was wealth. He asks a wizard to grant him a wish. He wishes that everything he touched would turn to gold. This also included food and he almost starved to death. Even King Midas' daughter turned to gold. In this scene, he is talking to a wizard).

<u>King Midas:</u>

I want more gold. I know I have a lot of gold. But gold is the best thing in the world! I want more! I wish that everything I touched would turn to gold. I don't care if it will not make me happy. I will take the risk.

(King Midas woke up the next day to find everything he touched, turned to gold).

My bed has turned to gold. My chair and table has turned to gold. Everything is turning to shining, yellow gold.

I'm hungry. I need a drink. Oh, my glass has turned to gold! The bread and even the meat have turned to gold!

Good morning Daughter, come here. I love you very much. Let me hug you. *(His daughter turns into a gold statue).* Oh no! You can't move. What have I done?

Wizard, please take away this horrible gift! Take all my gold. Take all my money. Take everything. Just give me back my daughter! I hate gold! I don't want any more of it! I'm sure. I don't want any more of it. I've learned my lesson. I don't think gold is the greatest thing in the world.

What should I do? You are telling me to run to the river and fill a pitcher with water and sprinkle it over everything that is gold? Yes, I can do that! Of course!

(King Midas runs to fetch a pitcher of water and eagerly sprinkles it over everything that he has turned to gold, starting with his precious daughter).

My daughter, you can move. *(He hugs her).* Now let us eat and be truly happy!

THE LION, THE WITCH & THE WARDROBE
BY C.S. LEWIS

(This is from the 2nd book of The Chronicles of Narnia. Mr Tumnus is a faun who lives in Narnia. In this scene he meets Lucy, the youngest of the four children in the story).

Mr Tumnus:

Good evening, good evening. Excuse me – I don't want to be inquisitive – but should I be right in thinking that you are a Daughter of Eve? Lucy? Forgive me – you are what they call a girl? You are in fact, Human? To be sure, to be sure, how stupid of me! But I've never seen a Son of Adam or a Daughter of Eve before. I am delighted. That is to say – Delighted, delighted! Allow me to introduce myself. My name is Tumnus. And may I ask, O Lucy, Daughter of Eve, how you have come into Narnia? This is the land of Narnia where we are now; all that lies between the lamppost and the great castle of Cair Paravel on the eastern sea. And you – you have come from the wild woods of the west?

(Lucy tells Mr Tumnus that she has come through the wardrobe).
Ah, if only I had worked harder at geography when I was a little Faun, I should no doubt know all about those strange countries. It is too late now.

It is winter in Narnia and has been for ever so long, and we shall both catch cold if we stand here talking in the snow. Daughter of Eve from the far land of Spare Oom where eternal summer reigns around the bright city of War Drobe, how would it be if you came and had tea with me? It's only just around the corner, and there'll be a roaring fire – and toast – sardines – cake.

If you will take my arm, Daughter of Eve, I shall be able to hold the umbrella over both of us. That's the way. Now – off we go. We shan't be long. *(Mr Tumnus takes Lucy into a little, dry, cave where he lives).*

THE LION, THE WITCH & THE WARDROBE BY C.S. LEWIS

(This is from the 2nd book of The Chronicles of Narnia. Edmund is in the land of Narnia. He comes face to face with the statue of a great lion. Edmund is under the influence of the White Witch and is visiting her house to give her information about her brother and sister. There is a courtyard full of creatures turned to stone).

Edmund:

This is the great lion Aslan they were all talking about. A lion! Why is it standing so still? His head is all covered with snow. It's only a statue. Cold stone! So, this is the Great Aslan! She has caught him already and turned him into stone. Who is afraid of Aslan now? Silly old Aslan. How do you like being a statue? You thought yourself mighty fine, didn't you? *(Edmund walks around the statues)*. Only stone!

(Suddenly Maugrim, the Queen's wolf appears, live and in person).

Oh! If you please, sir. My name is Edmund. I am the Son of Adam her Majesty met in the wood the other day and I've come to bring her the news that my brother and sisters are now in Narnia – quite close and at the Beavers' house. She wanted to see them. Will you tell Her Majesty that I am here.

(Maugrim takes Edmund to see the White Witch).

I'm come your Majesty. Please your Majesty, I've done the best I can. I've brought them quite close. They're in the little house on top of the dam just up the river – with Mr and Mrs Beaver. They say that Aslan is on the move. They're going to meet at the Stone Table. Please, your Majesty, I'm only repeating what they said.

THE LION, THE WITCH & THE WARDROBE
BY C.S. LEWIS

(This is from the 2nd book of The Chronicles of Narnia. Mr Beaver takes the four children back to his home in the dam. Mrs Beaver gives the children something to eat whilst Mr Beaver informs the children about the grave situation in Narnia).

<u>Mr Beaver:</u>

That's a very bad business indeed. Poor Mr Tumnus was taken off by the police. I got that from a bird who saw it done. They were heading northwards when they were last seen. It means they were taking him to *her* house. And there's not many taken in there that ever comes out again. Statues. All full of statues they say it is – in the courtyard and up the stairs and in the hall. People she's turned – turned into stone. I don't doubt you would save him if you could but you've no chance of getting into *that* house against her will and ever coming out alive. It's no good, Son of Adam, no good your trying. But now that Aslan is on the move –

Aslan? Why, don't you know? He's the King. He's the Lord of the whole wood, but he's not often here, you understand. Never in my time or my father's time. But the word has reached us that he has come back. He is in Narnia at this moment. He'll settle the White Queen all right. It is he, not you, that will save Mr Tumnus.

Lord love you, Son of Adam, what a simple thing to say! Turn *him* into stone? If she can stand on her two feet and look him in the face it'll be the most she can do and more than I expect of her. No, no. He'll put all to rights as it says in an old rhyme in these parts:

Wrong will be right, when Aslan comes in sight,
At the sound of his roar, sorrows will be no more,
When he bares his teeth, winter meets its death,
And when he shakes his mane,
we shall have spring again.

You'll understand when you see him. Daughter of Eve, that's what I brought you here for. I'm to lead you to where you shall meet him. Aslan, a man! Certainly not. I tell you he is the King of the wood and the son of the great Emperor-beyond-the-Sea. Don't you know who is the King of Beasts? Aslan is a lion – *the* Lion, the great Lion. But he isn't safe. But he's good. He's the King, I tell you. You shall see him. Word has been sent that you are to meet him, tomorrow if you can, at the Stone Table.

THE VOYAGE OF THE DAWN TREADER
BY C.S. LEWIS

(This is from the 5th book of The Chronicles of Narnia. Eustace is the unlikeable cousin of the Peter, Susan, Lucy and Edmund. He has travelled through the picture and has landed on an island).

Eustace:

First a picture comes to life. Then I'm half-drowned. Then I'm dragged aboard that horrible looking ship to meet a bunch of real wierdo's. I get attacked by a mouse. Then I'm sold as a slave. And finally shipwrecked on this awful looking island. Well, one thing's for sure, I'm never going back on the *Dawn Treader* again. Never, ever again. I hope it's so badly damaged that it never puts to sea again. There must be a British Consul somewhere. There's always a British Consul. Whenever you're in trouble abroad, go to the British Consul. That's what Ma and Pa say. So, it must be true. And what about that dreadful storm? I hate the sea. I'd much rather fly. I love flying. It's much safer. And quicker. Why, the crew of that awful ship hadn't even got emergency rockets or a radio to call for help. All they did was yell for Aslan, whatever that may mean. Aslan! Aslan! What a silly name! But at least I've got away from that nasty little mouse. He really hurt me with that spiky little sword of his. Ooh, I can still feel it. I detest that Reepicheep. He's not a mouse, he's a rat. A rotten little rat. Oh, where's this British Consul? What's that over there? It looks like smoke. And where there's smoke, there's fire. That's what Ma and Pa always say. A nice, warm fire to dry me out. And I won't tell the others.

(Eustace explores a little and finds a gold coin).

What's that? It's a coin. A gold coin! Gold! There's some more! Yes, look. Here. And here. And here. And those look like jewels. Look at this beautiful armlet. Why, this cave is full of treasure. I've found a treasure cave! And finder's-keepers. It's mine, all mine! Now I'll show everyone who's really in charge. What's that? Ugh! That's disgusting . . . *(Right in front of him is a huge sleeping dragon).*

GREAT EXPECTATIONS
BY CHARLES DICKENS

(Young Pip has been caught by an escaped convict and pleads for his life. The convict makes Pip promise to return with some wittles and a file the next morning to help him escape).

<u>Pip:</u>

Don't cut my throat, sir. Pray don't do it, sir. My name's Pip, sir. P-p-ip, sir!

That's where I live, sir. That's our village, on the flat in-shore among the alder-trees and pollards, a mile or more from the church. *(The convict turns Pip upside down, scaring the life out of him).*

My mother? There, sir. *(Pip points to his mother's grave).* Also, Georgiana. That's my mother. And my father too, sir. Late of this parish. I live with my sister, sir – Mrs Joe Gargery – wife of Joe Gargery, the blacksmith, sir. Yes, sir, I know what a file is. And I know what wittles is, yes, sir. I'll bring 'em both to you, sir.

If you would kindly please let me keep upright, sir, perhaps I shouldn't be sick, and perhaps I could attend more.

I'll bring them tomorrow morning early. I'll get you the file and I'll get you what broken bits of food I can, and I'll come to you at the Battery, early in the morning. Good night, sir.

(Pip runs off, picking his way among the nettles and brambles).

HARD TIMES
BY CHARLES DICKENS

(Tom confides in his sister, Louisa Gradgrind).

Tom Gradgrind:

I am sick of my life, Louisa. I hate it altogether, and I hate everybody except you ... I am a Donkey, that's what I am. I am as obstinate as one, I am more stupid than one, I get as much pleasure as one, and I should like to kick like one ... not you, Louisa. I wouldn't hurt you. I made an exception of you at first. I don't know what this – jolly old, jaundiced jail – would be without you. You are a girl, Louisa, and a girl comes out of it better than a boy does. You are the only pleasure I have – you can brighten even this place – and you can always lead me as you like ... I wish I could collect all the Facts we hear so much about, and all the Figures, and all the people who found them out: and I wish I could put a thousand barrels of gunpowder under them and blow them all up together! However, when I go to live with old Bounderby, I'll have my revenge. I mean, I'll enjoy myself a little, and go about and see something and hear something. I'll recompense myself for the way in which I've been brought up ... I shall very well know how to manage and smooth old Bounderby! ... And if that's a secret, it's not far off. It's you ... You are his little pet, you are his favourite; he'll do anything for you. When he says to me things I don't like, I shall say to him, 'My sister Lou will be hurt and disappointed, Mr Bounderby. She always used to tell me she was sure you would be easier with me than this. That'll bring him about, or nothing will ... Have you gone to sleep, Louisa? ... you seem to find more to look at in that fire than ever I could find. Another of the advantages, I suppose, of being a girl.

OLIVER
BY CHARLES DICKENS

(Oliver has run away from the Undertakers shop where he was treated very badly. On his travels, he meets Dodger, also known as Jack Dawkins, who introduces him to Fagin. Dodger is a cheeky Cockney boy).

<u>Dodger:</u>

Hullo, my covey! What's the row?
Walking for seven days! Oh, I see. Beak's order, eh? I suppose you don't know what a beak is, my flash com-pan-ion. My eyes, how green! Why, a beak's madgst'rate, and when you walk by a beak's order, it's not straight forward, but always agoing up, and never a coming down again. Was you never on the mill?

What mill! Why, *the* mill – the mill as takes up so little room that it'll work inside a Stone Jug; and always goes better when the wind's low with people, than when it's high, becos' then they can't get workmen. But come, you want grub, and you shall have it. I'm at low-water mark myself – only one bob and a magpie; but, as far as it goes, I'll fork out and stump. Up with you on your pins.

Going to London? Got any lodgings? Money?

Yes, I live in London when I'm at home. I suppose you want some place to sleep in tonight, don't you? Don't fret your eyelids on that score, I've got to be in London tonight, and I know a respectable old gentleman as lives there, wot'll give you lodgings for nothing, and never ask for the change – that is, if any gentleman he knows interduces you. And don't he know me? Oh, no! Not in the least! By no means. Certainly not!

(Jack takes him to the door of a house near Field Lane).

Whatcha, mate! A new pal! Where did he come from? Greenland! (*sarcastically*) Is Fagin upstairs?

(They enter and go upstairs. Jack introduces Oliver to Fagin.)

This is him, Fagin, my friend, Oliver Twist.

OLIVER TWIST
BY CHARLES DICKENS.

(Jack Dawkins, otherwise known as the Dodger, has befriended the innocent young Oliver Twist and is trying to persuade him to stay with Fagin and continue in the 'trade' of the rest of the boys – thieving!).

<u>Dodger</u>:

I suppose you don't even know what a prig is? I am and I'd scorn to be anything else. So is Charley and so is Fagin and Sykes and Nancy and Bet. We all are. Why don't you put yourself under Fagin, Oliver? And make a fortune out of hand? And be able to retire in your own property and be genteel. Go! Why, where's your spirit? Don't you take any pride out of yourself? Would you go and be dependent on your friends? Look at all this

(He shows Oliver lots of coins).

Here's a jolly life! Here, catch hold; there's plenty more where they were came from. You've been brought up bad. Fagin will make something of you, or you'll be the first he ever had that turned out unprofitable. You'd better begin at once, for you'll come to the trade long before you think of it; and you're only losing time, Oliver. If you don't take pocket handkerchiefs and watches, some other cove will; you've just as good a right to them as they have, Oliver!

A CHRISTMAS CAROL
BY CHARLES DICKENS

(Scrooge's nephew is talking to Scrooge about the joys of Christmas).

Nephew:

Christmas a humbug, Uncle? You don't mean that, I'm sure. What right have you to be dismal? You're rich enough!

There are many things from which I might have derived good, by which I have not profited, I daresay ... Christmas among the rest. But I am sure I have always thought of Christmas time, when it has come round – apart from the veneration due to its sacred name and origin – as a good time; the only time I know of, in the long calendar of the year, when men and women seem by one consent to open their shut-up hearts freely. And therefore, Uncle, though it has never put a scrap of gold or silver in my pocket, I believe that it *has* done me good, and *will* do me good; and so, I say, God Bless It!

Don't be angry, Uncle! Come, take Christmas dinner with us tomorrow?

Why did I get married? Because I fell in love! Uncle, you came to see me before that happened. Why give it as a reason for not coming now? I want nothing from you; I ask nothing of you; why cannot we be friends?

I am sorry, with all my heart, to find you so resolute. We have never had any quarrel to which I have been a party. But I have made the trial in homage to Christmas, and I'll keep my Christmas humour to the last. So, A Merry Christmas, Uncle. And a Happy New Year!

THE SECRET GARDEN
BY FRANCES HODGSON BURNETT

(Dickon is Martha's brother. He is a local Yorkshire lad who has a way with animals and nature. Mary has befriended him through her maid, Martha. In this scene, Dickon meets Mary for the first time and Mary shares her secret about the Secret Garden with him).

Dickon:

Yes, I'm Dickon. And thou'rt, Miss Mary. *(He is looking at a robin).* I get up slow so as not to fright the robin. I can tell what the birds are sayin'. And they say a lot. I have a pet fox too. He's a bonnie one. And I play the flute. Yorkshire's full o' good songs – and dances. The world would not go round so well without dancin' and singin'. It's part of the love of life. I have a wee garden by our cottage where I plant wild things – snowdrops and yellow primroses. I'll help you make a garden. Spring is here, and this is the time. I'll buy thee some seeds if tha' likes and help tha' plant them. Where will we dig?

Yes, I can keep a secret. The birds wouldna love me if I told where they build their nests.

Yes, I know about the garden behind the wall. It's been locked up tight these ten years, it is, and the key buried. The robin has shown you the way. Now you have to find the door.

(Mary shows him the door for she has already found it).

Whee – th'art a smart one. No wonder the bird took a fancy to thee. I never thought I'd see this place.

(Mary gives him some money so that Dickon can buy some things to work on the garden).

Thank you, Miss Mary. I'll buy some things in the town this afternoon and be back in the morning. We can work here most days, till the crocuses and lilies burst into bloom.

THE SECRET GARDEN
BY FRANCES HODGSON BURNETT

(The scene takes place in Colin's bedroom. Colin has been crying and Mary has heard the crying and has entered his bedroom to find out what is the matter).

Colin:

Who – who are you? Are you a ghost?

Mary? I am Colin Craven. Who are you? Mr Craven is my father.

They don't like to talk about me. They wish I were dead. Come here. You are real, aren't you? I thought you might be a dream.

I am in bed because I am not well – and I have a headache. I cry a lot.

Do you live here? And you've come from India?

My father thinks I'll have a crooked back like his, but I know I shall die soon anyway. I hear the nurses whispering about it when they think I'm not listening. *(Mary asks Colin to turn over so that she can inspect his back).* No lump, or anything? Just my backbone? Sometimes I'm scared to sit up for fear I'll feel a lump coming. Then I'd scream myself to death.

My father hates me because my mother died when I was born. He hardly ever comes to see me. He hates the garden too because she died. It's just a garden she used to like. If she had lived, I don't think I'd be so ill. You've found a garden locked up, Mary? Well, I'm going to see that they find the key, and that the door is unlocked. I want to see the garden my mother liked. All the servants have to obey me here. They do what I say – Medlock, Martha, all of them.

What secret? It will be our secret? That sounds like fun. I've never had a secret. I don't think I'd mind going outdoors for that. This boy, Dickon, who knows all about gardens. Perhaps he would help us. There would just be the three of us – and Dickon's animals, of course.

I say, Mary. I just thought of something. You and I are cousins!

THE SECRET GARDEN
BY FRANCES HODGSON BURNETT

(Colin is Mr Craven's son. He has been bedridden for years as the family believe him to be incurable. Colin's cousin Mary has recently come to live at the Manor and has discovered she has a cousin. Colin is very demanding and lonely. In this scene, he is talking to Martha. Martha has a brother, Dickon, who has been helping Mary redesign the secret garden. Later Mary and Mrs Medlock enter).

Colin:

Get my dressing gown right away, Martha. I want to be sitting up and ready when Mary comes. I want Mary to come. I want her to be here at once. I want her here now.
Tell Dickon to go away.

(He lies down in his bed and turns his back on Martha).

I'm not getting up. *(He is groaning).* I've a headache and a backache and I feel terrible. Go away. I'm ill, I tell you. Go away! And take the medicine away! It *won't* make me feel better. Nothing Dr Sturgis does makes me feel better. It makes me feel worse. Dr Sturgis doesn't want me to get better. He wants me to die. He's Father's nephew, and if I die, he'll inherit the Manor.

Mary can help. She can help – but she won't. Let me alone. I feel awful.

(Mary enters, followed shortly by Mrs Medlock, the housekeeper).

Mary! I started to get up. Then Martha said you weren't coming.

I didn't want you later. I wanted you right then – and – my head started to ache. I'll make them send Dickon away if you stay with him and leave me here alone. I'm not selfish! I'm not. Dickon's selfish to take so much of your time. I'm not selfish because I'm ill. And there's a lump coming on my back. And I'm going to die besides. I can feel it! I can feel it! It's right there! It's there – growing bigger! Oh! Oh! I can feel it growing! I'm going to die! I can't stop. I can't! But I have a lump. I can feel it. I'll have a hump on my back forever! (*He is wailing now*). I know it's there. Can't you feel it near my shoulder?

Can't you feel it? Are you sure? (*He gradually begins to believe Mary*). Do you – do you think – I could live to grow up? I'm not taking Dr Sturgis' advice anymore. I want to go outdoors with you Mary, and perhaps we'll find the secret gard – (*He stops himself, realising he has sworn not to mention in front of anyone*).

I'm going out right away. Help me get dressed, Mrs Medlock. You must help me at once. You may put me in the wheelchair, and call the butler to push me out to the gardens. This is going to be the most fun I've ever had.

THE SNOW QUEEN
BY HANS CHRISTIAN ANDERSON (1844)

(This story has been adapted by Suria Magito & Rudolf Weil. It is a story of two friends, Kai and Gerda who are neigh-bours. Kai's grandmother tells the story of the Snow Queen and one night the Snow Queen visits them and lures Kai to go with her. As splinters of the troll mirror reach Kai's eyes, he becomes cruel. The Snow Queen kisses him and he turns to ice. Gerda goes in search for her friend. The storyteller in this opening scene, sets the scene).

Storyteller:

Snip! Snap! Snooper! Crippety-crappity – BOOM!

(To the audience)
Oooh! People! Thin ones ... Fat ones ... Old ones ... Young ones ... short ones, tall ones, and some in between.

I'm Mr Storyteller. I'm important too – for without storytellers there wouldn't be any good stories! Now, I'm going to tell you one about a clever boy called Kay and the Snow Queen, and how they go to her great Ice Palace in the snow, far, far, far ... Oh, it's a lovely story! Magic roses, fights, robbers ... Do you know I know all the stories in the world?

I hope we'll run the villain through and let his wicked blood gush through the palace dungeons! Do you know, if I were to tell you a hundred stories a day for a hundred days, I would still have hundreds to tell you! But this one especially! You want to hear my story, don't you? I'll show you the story as a play!

Behind that curtain sits a girl – Gerda and her friend, a boy named Kay. It's winter when the story begins ... Yes, I know how it begins, but I don't know how it's all going to end; for I haven't invented the end yet. I'll have to make it up as I go. I may even have to take part in it myself if Kay and Gerda get into trouble. Anyway! Here we go! The Story of The Snow Queen! Sh!

I think I hear Kay mending his sledge … and … yes! There it is now – the organ-grinder's tune as he plays down in the cold streets below … It's Gerda's favourite tune … and Granny's too. Sh! … (*and the Storyteller puts his fingers to his lips*).

PUSS IN BOOTS (1552)

(Puss in boots is originally from an Italian fable but is now known all over the world. A poor Miller sets out to seek his fortune with his loyal cat).

Miller's Son:

Oh dear! I don't think anyone was ever so unlucky as I am. There are my two brothers finely set up, the eldest with the mill that Father left him, and the next one with the donkey; now one of them can grind all the corn that they bring him from the village, and the other can cart the meal round; but they haven't any use for me, because Father left me nothing but his cat. Of course, it's a very good-natured cat, and can talk, too, which is more than most cats can do, but I don't see how it's going to get me a living, as he said it would do. And my brothers won't even give me any new clothes – only old meal-bags to patch my coat with. Oh, dear! (*The Miller's cat enters*). Well, Puss, what are we going to do to earn our living?

Set out to seek our fortunes? What can you do to help, poor Puss? Boots? You want my old boots and my bag? (*Puss takes the clothes and exits*).

I wonder what Puss wants with that bag? He usually seems to know what he's about. Perhaps Father was right when he said he was leaving me something better than either of my brothers would get. I wonder. (*Puss comes back in wearing the boots and with the bag strung around his shoulders*).

Puss in boots! Puss in boots! Servant to the Miller's son. And now, we'll set out to see the world together!

THE TINDER BOX
BY HANS CHRISTIAN ANDERSON

(The White Dog is befriending the audience).

White Dog:

Good evening. Cold night for the time of the year, isn't it? I'm not really supposed to be speaking to you, you know. I'm not supposed to appear in the play until the second scene. I'd get into trouble if anyone knew I was here, talking like this. But I did want to see you all and find out if there's anyone here that I especially like. (*The white dog looks out into the audience*). And there is too ... over there ... I like him. And, oh, I do like her ... and there ... and there ... and there! You are making it difficult! I like you all. I've never seen so many likeable people in one place. I'll wag my tail for you ... Oh, bother, I can't! Never mind. You'll see me again in the second scene ... assuming there's been no trouble! ... and I'll wag my tail then. I won't say why I'm doing it because I'm not supposed to speak at all, really. But you'll all know the reason. I'll be doing it because I do like you all so very much. Now I must go, before they catch me here. You're going to meet a poor young soldier, called Peter ... and a nasty old witch with her two unfortunate slaves ... then we shall meet again, and I'll wag my tail for all of you. And you'll know why!

WORZEL GUMMIDGE
BY B E TODD (1937)

(Worzel Gummidge is a loveable scarecrow. He speaks with a country accent. Worzel Gummidge introduces himself to Susan and tells her all about his visit to London).

Worzel:

I'm Worzel Gummidge. I chose the name this morning. My granfer's name was Bogle. How old am I? All manner of ages. My face is one age, and my feet are another, and my arms are the oldest of all. 'Tis usual with scarecrows. And it's a good way too. I get a lot of birthdays. One for my face and another for my middle and another for my hands and so on ... I've never walked about before. But I says to myself last night, when I was standing in Ten Acre Field, I says 'You ought to go about the world and see things, same as the rabbits do. What's the use of having smart legs if you don't use them? I thought I'd go to London, till I met a mouse in the lane and she changed my mind for me. She had been to London herself. She was a field mouse and she'd heard tell of stowaways. So, she stowed herself away in a market basket and she saw Piccadilly – she saw a policeman and he was dressed just the same as the one in Scatterbrook, and she said if they couldn't do better than that in Piccadilly, she'd come home again. And she said they told such lies. There's a place they call St Martin in the Fields, and it isn't in the fields at all. There is another place called Shepherd's Market, and she said there wasn't a shepherd there. So, she said London was all a sham, and that it was trying to copy Scatterbrook, so she came home again!

TOAD OF TOAD HALL
BY KENNETH GRAHAME

(Rat lives on the riverbank. He is talking to Mole about the joys of the riverbank).

Rat:

Hallo Mole! Don't seem to have seen you about before. Prefer home-life? I know. Very good thing too in its way.

This is the river. *The* river. Never seen a – You never – Well, I – what *have* you been doing then?

My dear young friend, believe me, it's the *only* thing. There is *nothing* – absolutely nothing – so much worth doing as simply messing – messing about by a river – or *in* a river – or *on* a river. It doesn't matter which.

Do? Nothing. Just mess about. That's the charm of it; you're always busy, and yet you never do anything in particular; and when you've done it, there's always something else to do, and you can do it if you like, but you'd much better not … And so, you've never *seen* a river before? Well, well! I live by it, and with it and on it and in it. It's brother and sister to me, and aunts and company, and food and drink, and naturally – washing. It's my world, and I don't want any other. You're new to it. But believe me, my dear young friend, the Riverbank is so crowded nowadays that many people are moving away altogether. Otters, kingfishers, dabchicks, moorhens – No one else to – Oh, my dear young friend! No, no, I don't think you are very ignorant. Look here, Mole, what are you doing today?

Well, what I was about to suggest was a trifle of lunch on the bank here, and then I'd take you round and introduce you to a few of my friends. Does that appeal to you at all? There, there! You don't want to get *too* excited. It's only just a trifle of lunch. Cold tongue – cold ham – cold chicken – salad – French rolls – cress sandwiches – hard-boiled eggs – bloater paste – tinned peaches – meringues – ginger beer – lemonade – milk – chocolate – oranges – Nothing special – only just – Now just you wait here – don't go falling into the river or anything like that – and I'll be back in two minutes with the luncheon-basket.

TOAD OF TOAD HALL
BY KENNETH GRAHAME

(The Wild Wood. Mole is terrified alone in the wild wood until Ratty comes to the rescue).

Mole:

(Hopefully) Ratty! *(in a sudden panic)* What's that? *(The movement stops).* Pooh! It's nothing! I'm not frightened! ... I do wish Ratty were here. He's so comforting, is Ratty. Or the brave Mr Toad. He'd frighten them all away. *(He hears the sound of mocking laughter).* What's that? *(He looks around anxiously).* Ratty always said, 'Don't go into the Wild Wood.' That's what he always said. 'Not by yourself,' he said. 'It isn't safe,' he said. 'We never do,' he said. That's what Ratty said. But I thought I knew better. There he was, dear old Rat, dozing in front of the fire, and I thought if I just slipped out, just to see what the Wild Wood was like – *(He breaks off suddenly and darts round, fearing an attack from behind. There is nothing).* I should be safer up against a tree. Why didn't I think of that before? *(He settles himself at the foot of a tree).* Ratty would have thought of it, he's so wise. Oh, Ratty, I wish you were here! It's so much more friendly with two!

(He hears a voice from far off).

What's that? Who is it?

(Rat appears; a lantern in his hand, a couple of pistols in his belt, and a cudgel over his shoulder).

Oh, Rat! Oh, Rat! Oh, Ratty, I've been so frightened, you can't think. You've come by yourself. That's because you're so brave. Oh, Rat! It is comforting to hear somebody laugh again. Oh, Ratty. I don't know how to tell you, and I'm afraid you'll never want me for a companion again but I can't, I simply can't go all that way now. I'm tired. I'm aching all over. Oh, Ratty, do forgive me. I feel as if I must just sit here for ever and ever and ever, and I'm not a bit frightened now you're with me – and – and I think I want to go to sleep.

TOAD OF TOAD HALL
BY KENNETH GRAHAME

(A 'poop-poop' from a motor-car is heard, followed by a loud crash. Poor old toad, now out of his car, is a bit dazed. Rat supports Toad and takes him to a grassy bank to sit down. Mole is with them. Toad is a bit confused and thinks he's the motor-car).

Toad:

Poop-poop! ... Poop-poop! ... Poop-poop!

Poop-poop! ... Glorious, stirring sight! The poetry of motion! The real way to travel! The only way to travel! Here today – in the middle of next week tomorrow! Villages skipped, towns and cities jumped – always somebody else's towns and cities jumped – always somebody else's horizon. Oh bliss, oh rapture! Oh, poop-poop!

And to think I never knew! All those wasted years that lie behind me, I never knew, never even dreamt. But now that I know, now that I fully realize – ah, now! Oh, what a flowery track lies spread before me henceforth! What savoury dust-clouds shall spring up behind me as I speed on my reckless way, what luscious and entrancing smells. What cars I shall fling carelessly into the ditch in the wake of my magnificent onset. Horrid little carts – common carts – canary-coloured carts!

Police-station, Toad? Complaint! Me complain of that beautiful, that heavenly vision which has been vouchsafed me? Mend the cart? I've done with carts forever. Horrid little carts, common carts, canary-coloured carts!

Oh, Ratty! Oh, my good friend Mr Mole! You can't think how obliged I am to you for coming with me on this glorious trip. I wouldn't have gone without you, and then I might never have seen that – that swan, that star, that thunderbolt. I might never have heard that entrancing sound, nor smelt that bewitching smell! I owe it all to you, my dear, my very dear friends.

Poop-poop! Poop-poop! *(Rat and Mole take Toad home safely).*

TOAD OF TOAD HALL
BY KENNETH GRAHAME

(Rat and Mole arrive at Badger's house to discuss their friend Toad and his many calamities with motorcars. Later, Toad arrives himself).

Badger:

Well, well, well! Rat and his friend Mole! *(He escorts them in).* Come along in, both of you, at once. Why, you must be perished! Well, I never! Lost in the snow! And your friend that tired! Well, well, well! And in the Wild Wood at this time of night! *(He pats their heads paternally).* I'm afraid you've been up to some of your pranks again, Ratty. But come along in. There's a good fire here, and supper and everything.

Now, what will you do first? Toast your toes a bit? *(He removes The Times newspaper).* I was just glancing at the paper. Or supper now, and toast your toes afterwards? It's all ready. I was expecting one or two friends might drop in. Won't you try a pickle?

I've been wanting to see you fellows, because I have heard very grave reports of our mutual friend, Toad. Is his case as hopeless as one has heard? How many smash-ups has he had? Alas, alas! I knew his father. I knew his grandfather. Alas, poor witless animal!

At any moment another new and exceptionally powerful motorcar will arrive at Toad hall for approval or return. We must be up and going before it is too late.

The first step is to get him here and reason with him. You know how it is. In the present weather, I don't go about much. Naturally. Let us apply our minds to it.

(Suddenly the bell rings loudly)
Whoever's that?

(Toad falls into Badger's arms, panting with fear).

Won't you sit down, Toad? (*Solemnly*). Toad, I knew your father, worthy animal that he was; I knew your grandfather. It was also my privilege to be slightly acquainted with your uncle, the Archdeacon; of that I shall speak further directly. The question I wish to ask you now is this. At the beginning of the breathless story of adventure to which we have just been listening, you mentioned *(He pauses dramatically)* a motorcar. You implied further that this motorcar had suddenly lost its efficiency. Am I right in supposing that just at this moment your narrative hovered for an instant on the confines of truth?

I asked you, Toad, if it is indeed a fact that your eighth motorcar is now in as fragmentary a condition as the previous seven? *(Toad agrees with Badger)*. Toad! Rise from your chair a moment. (*Toad rises*). Rat, Mole, may I trouble you a moment? *(Rat & Mole place a chair for Toad so that they can cross-examine him)*. Thankyou. Now then, Toad, first of all take those ridiculous goggles off. *(As Toad refuses, Rat and Mole remove his goggles)*. That is better.

Now then, Toad. You've disregarded all the warnings we've given you. You've gone on squandering the money your father left you, and you're getting us animals a bad name in the district by your furious driving and your smashes and your rows with the police. We have decided, my friend Ratty here and Mole and I, that it is time we saved you from yourself. I am going to make one more effort to bring you to reason. You will come with me into my study, and there you will hear some facts about yourself. I say the study, because on second thoughts I have decided, for the sake of your revered grandfather, to spare you the pain of a public reproof. Come!

TOAD OF TOAD HALL
BY KENNETH GRAHAME

(Toad finds himself at the Court House in front of a Judge and jury after stealing a motorcar. This is his defense).

Toad:

Here I am. I don't want to be tried!

I wasn't driving recklessly, I was just going along quietly at about seventy miles an hour, when I saw this policeman in front of me. Naturally, I quickened up to see if he wanted anything. Same as anyone else would have done, who's fond of policemen.

What did I call you, officer? Well, I can't remember … I didn't mean him more than anyone else. I just murmured the expression to myself … I'm that sort of person. It's a result of my artistic temperament … The car? … Oh, yes, the car … Well, I didn't mean to steal it. It was this way. I was just having a bit of lunch at an inn. You see, I'd been very ill … hadn't I, Ratty? … and my dear friends were looking after me. Well, we were just having a bit of lunch at an inn. It was the first time I'd been up and out, just a round of beef and a few pickled walnuts and a couple of helpings of treacle pudding – when suddenly I hear Poop, Poop, Poop … Oh, it's just an imitation of a car, your Honour. So, I went outside to have a look – as anyone would. I thought there couldn't be any harm in my only just looking at it. So, I looked at it and then naturally – I say to myself, I wonder if it starts … so I wound it up, and it did … then I said … I wonder if it goes … so I just sat in the driver's seat … and it did go … then I saw this policeman with a fat … I mean with such a nice face who said, 'You're going at 170 miles an hour'. So, I said to this handsome policeman … Well, of course, if you say so, dear Mr Policeman …

(Toad is sentenced to 20 years imprisonment).
Twenty years ... you're going to sentence me for twenty years in prison ... Well ... I think you're all fat faces. All of you! The whole lot of you! I'm Toad ... the Terror of the Highway. Toad the Traffic-queller. I am Toad the handsome, the popular, the successful ... and what are you? Just fat-faces ... all of you, just fat-faces!

TOAD OF TOAD HALL
BY KENNETH GRAHAME

(In the Banqueting room of Toad Hall. The weasels have taken over Toad Hall. It is the Chief Weasel's birthday and a banquet is in progress. The Chief Weasel is sitting at the head of the main table with a laurel wreath on his head).

<u>Chief Weasel:</u>

Friends and Fellow Animals. Before we part this evening, I have one final toast to propose. *(Everyone cheers 'Hear, Hear!).* It is a toast which on all occasions have something of solemnity in it, something even of sadness, but never more so than on this occasion. 'Absent Friends.' *(Hear, Hear).* Absent Friends. With this toast I couple first the name of our kind host, Mr Toad. *(Loud laughter).* Although, unable to be present himself tonight – owing to a previous engagement – Mr Toad has generously put his entire establishment at our disposal for as long as we like to make use of it. *(Loud laughter).* We all know Toad – good Toad, wise Toad, modest Toad. It is a personal sorrow to every one of us that he is not amongst us tonight.

But while we are thinking of our good host, Mr Toad, we must not forget our other absent friends – Mr Badger, Mr Rat and Mr Mole. *(Laughter).* It is a particular sorrow to me that they are not with us tonight, living as they do – unlike Mr Toad – so very conveniently in the neighborhood. From time to time, indeed, of late, we have caught glimpses of them – behind hedges. We have seen their back views – in the distance – they cannot plead absence from the country as an excuse for their absence from our board, so that the only reason for it must be excessive shyness. *(Laughter).* Modesty. *(Laughter).* All the more, do we regret that they did not see fit to join us. Fellow animals, I give you the toast – 'Absent Friends!'

(After Chief Weasel has made this speech in mockery of Toad and his friends, Badger, Mole and Toad rush in to re-claim Toad Hall).

THE HOUSE AT POOH CORNER
BY A. A. MILNE

(Eeyore has written a poem).

<u>Eeyore:</u>

Don't bustle me. Don't now-then me. Nobody knows anything about this. This is a surprise. (*Eeyore takes a piece of paper from behind his ear).*
What-nots and Etceteras, before I begin, or perhaps I should say, before I end, I have a piece of Poetry to read to you. Hitherto – hitherto – a long word meaning – well, you'll see what it means directly – hitherto, as I was saying, all the Poetry in the Forest has been written by Pooh, a Bear with a Pleasing Manner but a Positively Startling Lack of Brain. The Poem which I am now about to read to you was written by Eeyore, or Myself, in a Quiet Moment. If somebody will take Roo's bull's eye away from him, and wake up Owl, we shall all be able to enjoy it. I call it – Poem. This was is.

Christopher Robin is going.
At least I think he is.
Where?
Nobody knows.
But he is going –
I mean he goes
(To rhyme with knows)
Do we care?
(To rhyme with where)
We do
Very much.
(I haven't got a rhyme for that 'is' in the second line yet. Bother).
(Now I haven't got a rhyme for bother. Bother).
Those two bothers will have to rhyme with each other
The fact is this is more difficult than I thought,

I ought
To begin again,
But it is easier
To stop.
Christopher Robin, goodbye.
I
(Good)
I
And all your friends
Sends –
I mean all your friends
Send –
(Very awkward this, it keeps going wrong)
Well, anyhow, we send
Our love.
End.

If anybody wants to clap, now is the time to do it …
Thankyou. Unexpected and gratifying, if a little lacking in smack!

TOM SAWYER
BY MARK TWAIN

(Ever resourceful, Tom Sawyer, to find a way to get out of painting Aunt Polly's fence).

Tom:

It's just not fair. It's a lovely morning. Just the day to go fishing! Look at that fence! Thirty yards and nine foot high! I'll never finish it.

I shall be the laughingstock of the town. I *must* try and find a way out of it.

I haven't even got enough things to trade! A marble ... a broken toy ... just trash! Wait a moment! I've got a plan ... a really good plan! There's Ben Rogers now. I'll try it out on him.

Hmmmm.... He's not even seen me yet. I like the look of the apple he's eating. A big, juicy one! Ah! He's seen me. Now, I'll pretend not to have seen him.

Why, it's you, Ben. I didn't notice! Are you going swimming? Work! You think I've got to work? This isn't work, it's really interesting and I like it! Does a boy get the chance to whitewash a fence every day? Just watch me and see what I mean. Do you want a go? No ... no, I reckon it would hardly do. You see, Aunt Polly's very particular about this fence because it's on the street. It would have been different if it was the back fence ... but, it's got to be done very carefully. I reckon there isn't one boy in a thousand – maybe two thousand – that could do it the way it's got to be done! Jim and Sid wanted to do it but she wouldn't let them. So, you see how I'm fixed! If you did tackle this fence and anything happened to it ... Well, I suppose I might let you ... if you were to give me your apple... The whole of it! (*Ben gives Tom the apple*).What a pushover! That was easy! I'll soon get it finished this way. I'll get all the boys wanting to take a turn and I'll get some treasures to keep as well!

PINOCCHIO
BY CARLO COLLODI (1883)

(Gepetto is talking to his neigh-bour, a carpenter, named Master Antonio. He tells him he plans to make a puppet. Antonio gives him some wood which seems to have a 'life of its own'. As soon as Gepetto has finished the puppet, it starts to come to life and behaves very badly. In this scene, Gepetto is being stared at by two wooden eyes).

<u>Gepetto:</u>

This morning an idea came into my head. I thought I would make a beautiful wooden puppet; one that could dance, fence, and leap like an acrobat. With this puppet I would travel about the world to earn a piece of bread and a glass of wine. I want a little wood to make my puppet; will you give me some?

What name shall I give him? I think I will call him Pinocchio.

Wicked wooden eyes, why do you look at me?

I've no sooner carved your nose and it has began to grow. And grow and grow and grow!

And your mouth. Stop laughing! Stop laughing, I say!

Pinocchio! Give me back my wig instantly! You young rascal! You are not yet completed and you are already beginning to show want of respect to your father! That is bad, my boy, very bad! *(Gepetto cries a little, in desperation. When he has finished making the puppet's feet, he is kicked by the puppet).*

Ouch! I deserve it! I should have thought of it sooner! Now it is too late! I'd better teach him to walk.

Stop him! Stop him! (*Pinocchio runs away*).

Wretched boy! And to think how I laboured to make him a well-conducted puppet! But it serves me right! I should have thought of it sooner!

PINOCCHIO
BY CARLO COLLODI (1883)

(Pinocchio is on his way to school for the first time).

Pinocchio:

At school today I shall learn to read in no time; tomorrow I shall learn to write and then, the day after tomorrow, I shall learn how to add up and take away. Soon I will be clever enough to earn lots and lots of money, and with my very first money I shall buy Gepetto the best and warmest coat I can find, made of fine cloth. No. It won't be a cloth coat. It shall be made of gold and silver with sparkling diamond buttons. My poor Daddy deserves the best – because he sold his coat to buy me this book for school – and now he has no coat, and in this cold weather too!

(He hears music playing)

Where is that music coming from, I wonder – and who is playing it? What a shame I have to go to school – otherwise – I know! Today, I'll go and listen to the music and tomorrow I'll go to school! That's a good idea!

PINOCCHIO
BY CARLO COLLODI (1883)

(Pinocchio returns home from his travels only because he is hungry. Geppetto, Pinocchio's father, offers Pinocchio his own breakfast).

Pinocchio:

Dear papa, I cannot open the door! Because my feet have been eaten.

The cat ate my feet! *(He is lying).*

I cannot stand up, believe me. Oh, poor me! Poor me! I shall have to walk on my knees for the rest of my life! *(Geppetto takes pity on Pinocchio).*

I don't know how I managed to burn my feet, papa, but it has been such a dreadful night that I shall remember it as long as I live. It thundered and lightened, and I was very hungry, and then the Talking-Cricket said to me: 'It serves you right; you have been wicked and you deserve it' and I said to him: 'Take care, Cricket!' and he said: 'You are a puppet and you have a wooden head,' and I threw the handle of a hammer at him, and he died, but the fault was his, for I didn't wish to kill him, and the proof of it is that I put an earthenware saucer on a brazier of burning embers, but a chicken flew out and said: 'Adieu until we meet again, and many compliments to all at home': and I got still more hungry, for which reason that little old man in a night-cap, opening the window, said to me: 'Come underneath and hold out your hat,' and poured a basinful of water on my head, because asking for a little bread isn't a disgrace, is it? And I returned home at once, and because I was always very hungry, I put my feet on the brazier to dry them, and then you returned, and I found they were burnt off, and I am always hungry, but I have no longer any feet! Oh! Oh! Oh! Oh!

Those three pears - If you wish me to eat them, be kind enough to peel them for me?

You are no doubt right but I will never eat fruit that has not been

peeled. I cannot bear rind.
(Geppetto peels the fruit for Pinocchio. When Pinocchio eats the fruit, he begins to throw away the core).

But core I am determined I will not eat even though I am as hungry as ever!

If you have nothing more to give me, I must have patience! If there is nothing else, I will eat a rind.

(He suddenly realises the core and the rind was not too bad).

Ah! Now I feel comfortable.

THE HAPPY PRINCE
BY OSCAR WILDE (1888)

(*This is Oscar Wilde's short story about the statue of the Happy Prince. He is set on a pedestal high above the city overlooking the city below. He befriends the Swallow who has decided to make the statue his home for one night. He is persuaded to spend several nights with the statue and is asked to carry out a series of tasks for the Prince. Over the course of a few days, the statue asks the swallow to redistribute his wealth. He distributes his ruby, his sapphires and his gold to those in need and, on the swallows' death, he becomes the Happy Prince*).

The Prince:

I am the Happy Prince. When I was alive and had a human heart, I did not know what tears were, for I lived in the Palace of Sans-Souci, where sorrow is not allowed to enter. In the days I played with my companions in the garden, and in the evening, I led the dance in the Great Hall. Round the garden ran a very lofty wall, but I never cared to ask what lay beyond it, everything about me was so beautiful. My courtiers called me the Happy Prince, and happy indeed I was, if pleasure be happiness. So, I lived, and so I died. And now that I am dead, they have set me up here so high that I can see all the ugliness and all the misery of my city, and though my heart is made of lead yet I cannot choose but weep. Far away, far away in a little street there is a poor house. One of the windows is open, and through it I can see a woman seated at a table. Her face is thin and worn, and she has coarse, red hands, all pricked by the needle, for she is a seamstress. She is embroidering passion flowers on a satin gown for the loveliest of the Queen's maids-of-honour to wear at the next Court ball. In a bed in the corner of the room her little boy is lying ill. He has a fever and is asking for oranges. His mother has nothing to give him but river water, so he is crying. Swallow, Swallow, little Swallow, will you not bring her the ruby out of my sword-hilt? My feet are fastened to this pedestal and I cannot move. You will stay with me for one night and be my messenger? Thank you, little Swallow.

Far away across the city I see a young man in a garret. He is leaning over a desk covered with papers, and in a tumbler by his side there is a bunch of withered violets. His hair is brown and crisp, and his lips are red as a pomegranate, and he has large and dreamy eyes. He is trying to finish a play for the Director of the Theatre, but he is too cold to write any more. There is no fire in the grate, and hunger has made him faint. I have no rubies now, my eyes are all that I have left. They are made of rare sapphires, which were brought out of India a thousand years ago. Pluck out one of them and take it to him. He will sell it to the jeweler, and buy firewood, and finish his play.

In the square below, there stands a little match-girl. She has let her matches fall in the gutter, and they are all spoiled. Her father will beat her if she does not bring home some money, and she is crying. She has no shoes or stockings, and her little head is bare. Pluck out my other eye, and give it to her, and her father will not beat her. Do as I command you.

Dear little Swallow, you tell me of marvelous things, but more marvelous than anything is the suffering of men and of women. There is no Mystery so great as Misery. Fly over my city, little Swallow, and tell me what you see there. I am covered with fine gold, you must take it off, leaf by leaf, and give it to my poor; the living always think that gold can make them happy.

THE REMARKABLE ROCKET
BY OSCAR WILDE (1888)

(This short story is a parody of status, class and arrogance. There is to be a wedding between a prince and princess. Everyone is invited to the celebration and a huge firework display is arranged. The 'talking' fireworks' are dismayed by the pompous, 'remarkable' rocket who is full of arrogance and conceit. As he is too damp to alight, he is discarded over the castle walls. He is eventually found by two boys who collect him to use as kindling. When he is eventually put on to a fire, he explodes, and much to his dismay, there is no one of any importance to note his grandeur).

Rocket:

I am a remarkable rocket and come from remarkable parents. My mother was the most celebrated Catherine wheel of her day and was renowned for her graceful dancing. When she made her great public appearance, she spun around nineteen times before she went out, and each time she threw into the air seven pink stars. She was three feet and a half in diameter and made of the very best gunpowder. My father was a rocket like myself, and of French extraction. He flew so high that the people were afraid that he would never come down again. He did, though, and made a most brilliant descent in a shower of golden rain. The newspapers wrote about his performance in very flattering terms. Indeed, the Court Gazette called him a triumph of Pyrotechnic art!

(*The other fireworks laugh at him*).

Pray, what are you laughing at? I am not laughing What right have you to be happy? You should be thinking about me. I am always thinking about myself, and I expect everybody else to do the same. That is what you call sympathy. It is a beautiful virtue, and I possess it in a high degree. Suppose anything happened to me tonight, what a misfortune that would be for everyone! The Prince and Princess would never be happy again, their whole married life would be spoiled; and as for the King, I know he would not get over it. Really, when I begin to reflect on the importance of my position, I am almost moved to tears. You forget that I am very uncommon, and very remarkable. Why anybody can have common sense, provided that they have no imagination. But I have imagination, for I never think of things as they really are; I always think of them as being quite different. As for keeping myself dry, there is evidently no one here who can at all appreciate an emotional nature. Fortunately for myself, I don't care. The only thing that sustains one through life is the consciousness of the immense inferiority of everybody else, and this is a feeling I have always cultivated. But none of you has any hearts. Here you are laughing and making merry just as if the Prince and Princess had not just been married.

Just think – perhaps they may go to live in a country where there is a deep river, and perhaps they may have only one son, a little fair-haired boy with violet eyes like the Prince himself; and perhaps someday he may go out to walk with his nurse; and perhaps the nurse may go to sleep under a great elder-tree; and perhaps the little boy may fall into the deep river and be drowned. What a terrible misfortune! Poor people, to lose their only son! It really is too dreadful! I shall never get over it! I never said that they had, I said that they might. If they had lost their only son there would be no use in saying any more about the matter. I hate people who cry over spilt milk. But when I think that they might lose their only son, I certainly am very much affected.

THE REMARKABLE ROCKET
BY OSCAR WILDE (1888)

(This short story is a parody of status, class and arrogance. There is to be a wedding between a prince and princess. Everyone is invited to the celebration and a huge firework display is arranged. The 'talking' fireworks' are dismayed by the pompous, 'remarkable' rocket who is full of arrogance and conceit. As he is too damp to alight, he is discarded over the castle walls. He is eventually found by two boys who collect him as kindling. When he is eventually put on to a fire, he explodes, and much to his dismay there is no one of any importance to note his grandeur. In this scene, he has been thrown away and he tries to convince himself that he is only a visitor in the woods).

Rocket:

I am merely a visitor, a distinguished visitor. The fact is that I find this place rather tedious. There is neither society here, nor solitude. In fact, it is essentially suburban. I shall probably go back to Court, for I know that I am destined to make a sensation in the world. I am made for public life, and so are all my relations, even the humblest of them. Whenever we appear, we excite great attention. I have not actually appeared myself, but when I do so it will be a magnificent sight. As for domesticity, it ages one rapidly, and distracts one's mind from higher things.

(*He spots two boys playing in the woods*) Two little boys. This must be the deputation.

(*They describe him as an old stick*) OLD STICK! Impossible! GOLD STICK, that is what he said. Gold Stick is very complimentary. In fact, he mistakes me for one of the Court dignitaries! They are putting me on top of the fire. This is magnificent, they are going to let me off in broad daylight, so that everyone can see me.

(*The boys use him for kindling for their fire*).

Now I am going off! I know I shall go much higher than the stars, much higher than the moon, much higher than the sun. In fact, I shall go so high that –

Fizz! Fizz! Fizz! Delightful! I shall go on like this for ever. What a success I am!

Now I am going to explode, I shall set the whole world on fire, and make such a noise that nobody will talk about anything else for a whole year. Bang! Bang! Bang!

(*The rocket explodes with no one to witness his grandeur*).

ANDROCLES & THE LION
BY GEORGE BERNARD SHAW (1915)

(From the Prologue of the play. Androcles is in the jungle and has come face to face with a wounded lion. He tries to protect his wife, Megaera and ends up befriending the injured lion).

Androcles:

(keeping between the lion and his wife, Megaera).

Don't you come near my wife, do you hear?

Meggy, run. Run for your life. If I take my eye off him, it's all up.

(Androcles notices that the Lion has a thorn in his paw).

Oh, he's lame, poor old chap! He's got a thorn in his paw. A frightfully big thorn. Oh, poor old man! Did um get an awful thorn into um's tootsums wootsums? Has it made um too sick to eat a nice little Christian man for um's breakfast? Oh, a nice little Christian man will get um's thorn out for um; and then um shall eat the nice Christian man and the nice Christian man's nice big tender wifey pifey.

Now, now, um is not to bite and not to scratch, not even if it hurts a very very little. Now make velvet paws. That's right. Steadeeee! Oh, did the nasty cruel little Christian man hurt the sore paw?

Well, one more little pull and it will be all over. Oh, mustn't frighten um's good kind doctor, um's affectionate nursey.

That didn't hurt at all; not a bit. Just one more. Just to show how the brave big lion can bear pain, not like the little crybaby Christian man. Oops! That's it!
Now it's out. Now lick um's paw to take away the nasty inflammation. See?

Clever little liony-piony! Understands um's dear old friend Andy Wandy! Yes, kissums Andy Wandy. Velvet paws! Velvet paws! That's right.

(Androcles & the Lion start to dance round and round in a waltz and away through the jungle).

ANDROCLES & THE LION
BY GEORGE BERNARD SHAW (1915)

(Androcles, a Christian, has sacrificed himself for other Christians, and is being thrown to the lions. Fortunately for Androcles, the lion he once rescued, recognizes him. He is talking to the Emperor. The scene takes place in a Roman Amphitheatre).

<u>Androcles:</u>

(talking to the guards just before he is due to be thrown to the lions).

No: I should never have another happy hour. No: on the faith of a Christian and the honor of a tailor, I accept the lot that has fallen on me. If my wife turns up, give her my love and say that my wish was that she should be happy with her next, poor fellow! Caesar: go to your box and see how a tailor can die. Make way for number twelve there.

(Androcles is now in the Amphitheatre. The lion recognizes him).

Now I wonder why they all run away from us like that.

(The emperor is by now in the Amphitheatre. Androcles holds the lion back from the emperor).

Don't run away, sir. He can't help spring if you run. Don't be afraid of him. Never be afraid of animals, your worship: that's the great secret. He'll be as gentle as a lamb when he knows that you are his friend. Stand quite still; and smile; and let him smell you all over just to reassure him; for, you see, he's afraid of you; and he must examine you thoroughly before he gives you his confidence. Come now, Tommy; and speak nicely to the emperor, the great good Emperor who has power to have all our heads cut off if we don't behave very, very respectfully to him. *(The Lion attempts to chase the emperor).* Oh bad, wicked Tommy, to chase the emperor like that! Let go of the emperor's robe at once, sir; where are your manners? Don't pull it away from him, your worship. He's only playing. Now I shall be really angry with you, Tommy, if you don't let go. I'll tell you what it is, sir: he thinks you and I are not friends.

We mustn't let him lash himself into a rage. You must show him that you are my particular friend – if you will have the condescension.

Oh, don't talk like that, sir. He understands every word you say: all animals do: they take it from the tone of your voice. I think he's going to spring at your worship. If you wouldn't mind saying something affectionate.

(Androcles has the lion totally under control now).

There! You see, your worship, a child might play with him now. See! Come and pet him. Oh, sir, how few men would have the courage to do that!

Quite safe now, sir.

HEIDI
BY JOHANNA SPIRI (1880)

(Heidi has gong to live with her elderly grandfather in the mountains. She has met a boy called Peter who is a goatherd. He introduces the goats to Heidi).

Peter:

Where have you got to now, Heidi? Come along here! You are not to fall over the rocks, your grandfather gave orders that you were not to do so. The rocks are up above, right up above. We have a long way to go yet, so come along! And on the topmost peak of all, the old bird of prey sits and croaks. See the great bird is there – look, look! It's going home to its nest. No, we can't climb up there and see where his nest is, Heidi. Why even the goats cannot climb as high as that, besides didn't Uncle say that you were not to fall over the rocks. Here, have some bread and cheese and some delicious fresh milk from the white goat. The two large pieces of bread and cheese are yours also, and when you have drunk up that milk, you are to have another bowlful from the white goat and then it will be my turn. I get the milk from my own goat, the piebald one. But go on now with your dinner.

I'll tell you the goats names. That's the great Turk with his big horns, who always wants to butt the others so that most of them run away when they see him coming. They will have nothing to do with their rough companion. That's Greenfinch, the slender, nimble little goat who is brave enough to face him and will make a rush at him, three or four times in succession, with such agility and dexterity that the great Turk often stands still quite astounded and won't venture to attack her again. Then there's little White Snowflake, who bleats in such a plaintive and beseeching manner. She cries like that because the old goat is not with her; she was sold at Maienfeld the day before yesterday, and so will not be coming up the mountain anymore. And the old goat, that is her mother. The prettiest of all the goats are Little Swan and Little Bear. Alm-Uncle brushes them down and washes them and gives them salt, and he has the nicest shed for them.

Get up, we must go home now. You can come with me again tomorrow!

A MIDSUMMER NIGHT'S DREAM
BY WILLIAM SHAKESPEARE (1600)

(In Act 3, Sc 2, Puck tells us how he has administered the love potion into Titania's eyes)

<u>Puck:</u>

My mistress with a monster is in love.
Near to her close and consecrated bower
While she was in her dull and sleeping hour
A crew of patches, rude mechanicals
That work for bread upon Athenian stalls,
Were met together to rehearse a play
Intended for great Theseus' nuptial day.
The shallowest thickskin of that barren sort,
Who Pyramus presented, in their sport,
Forsook his scene and entered in a brake,
When I did him at this advantage take.
An ass's nole I fixed on his head.
Anon his Thisbe must be answered,
And forth my mimic comes. When they him spy –
As wild geese that the creeping fowler eye,
Or russet-pated choughs, many in sort,
Rising and cawing at the gun's report,
Sever themselves and madly sweep the sky –
So, at his sight, away his fellows fly;
And at our stamp here o'er and o'er one falls.
He "Murder" cries and help from Athens calls.
Their sense thus weak, lost with their fears thus strong,
Made senseless things begin to do them wrong.
For briers and thorns at their apparel snatch;
Some sleeves, some hats – from yielders all things catch.
I led them on in this distracted fear,
And left sweet Pyramus translated there;

When in that moment, so it came to pass,
Titania waked and straightway loved an ass.

HENRY 5TH
BY WILLIAM SHAKESPEARE (1600)

(This young boy, who is servant to three cowardly idiots, Bardolph, Pistol and Nym, has more sense than the three put together. He is most observant of their villainous characteristics and does not approve of their ill morals. The boy feels he should leave their employment. However, as young as he is, he does sadly have to join them on the battle fields and gets killed).

<u>Boy:</u>

As young as I am, I have observed these three swashers. I am boy to them all three, but all they three, though they should serve me, could not be man to me, for indeed three such antics do not amount to a man. For Bardolph, he is white-livered and red-faced – by the means whereof he faces it out but fights not. For Pistol, he hath a killing tongue and a quiet sword – by the means whereof he breaks words and keeps whole weapons. For Nim, he hath heard that men of few words are the best men, and therefore he scorns to say his prayers, lest he should be thought a coward. But his few bad words are matched with as few good deeds – for he never broke any man's head but his own, and that was against a post, when he was drunk. They will steal anything and call it "purchase". Bardolph stole a lute case, bore it twelve leagues, and sold it for three halfpence. Nim and Bardolph are sworn brothers in filching, and in Calais they stole a fire shovel. I knew by that piece of service the men would carry coals. They would have me as familiar with men's pockets as their gloves or their handkerchiefs – which makes much against my manhood, if I should take from another's pocket to put into mine, for it is plain pocketing up of wrongs. I must leave them and seek some better service. Their villainy goes against my weak stomach, and therefore, I must cast it up.

KING JOHN
BY WILLIAM SHAKESPEARE (1623)

(Prince Arthur is talking to Hubert. Arthur does not know that Hubert has been ordered to kill him).

Prince Arthur:

Good morrow, Hubert.
You are sad.
Mercy on me!
Methinks nobody should be sad but I.
Yet, I remember, when I was in France,
Young gentlemen would be as sad as night,
Only for wantoness. By my Christendom,
So I were out of prison and kept sheep,
I should be as merry as the day is long;
And so, I would be here but that I doubt
My uncle practices more harm to me;
He is afraid of me, and I of him.
Is it my fault that I was Geffrey's son?
No, indeed, is't not; and I would to heaven
I were your son, so you would love me, Herbert.

(Arthur notices that Hubert is reacting strangely, for Hubert has been ordered to kill the young Prince Arthur).

Are you sick, Hubert? You look pale today;
In sooth, I would you were a little sick,
That I might sit all night and watch with you.
I warrant I love you more than you do me.

THE MERCHANT OF VENICE
BY WILLIAM SHAKESPEARE (1600)

(In Act 2, Sc 2, Launcelot is Shylock's servant. In this scene, he is wrestling with his conscience whether to leave or remain in the Jew's employment)

Launcelot:

Certainly, my conscience will serve me to run from this Jew, my master. The fiend is at mine elbow, and tempts me, saying to me, Launcelot Gobbo, good Launcelot', or 'good Gobbo', or 'good Launcelot Gobbo use your legs, take the start, run away'. My conscience says, 'No, take heed honest Launcelot, take heed honest Gobbo,' or as aforesaid, honest Launcelot Gobbo; do not run, scorn running with thy heels'. Well, the most courageous fiend bids me pack: 'Fia!' says the fiend; 'away!' says the fiend; 'for the heavens, rouse up a brave mind', says the fiend, 'and run'. Well, my conscience, hanging about the neck of my heart, says very wisely to me: 'My honest friend Launcelot, being an honest man's son,' or rather an honest woman's son – for indeed my father did something smack, something grow to, he had a kind of taste – well, my conscience says, 'Launcelot budge not'. 'Budge', says the fiend. 'Budge not,' says my conscience. ''Conscience', say I, 'you counsel well.' 'Fiend', say I, 'you counsel well.' To be ruled by my conscience, I should stay with the Jew my master, who – god bless the mark – is a kind of devil; and to run away from the Jew I should be ruled by the fiend, who – saving your reverence – is the devil himself. Certainly, the Jew is the very devil incarnation, and in my conscience, my conscience is but a kind of hard conscience, to offer to counsel me to stay with the Jew. The fiend gives the more friendly counsel. I will run, fiend; my heels are at your command, I will run.

TWELFTH NIGHT
BY WILLIAM SHAKESPEARE (1602)

(In Act 4, Sc 3, Sebastian, on searching for his twin sister, Viola, has wandered into the Countess Olivia's garden. Olivia, supposing Sebastian is Viola, has given him a pearl as a token of her affection. Sebastian is completely bemused).

<u>Sebastian:</u>

This is the air, that is the glorious Sun,
This pearl she gave me. I do feel't, and see't,
And though 'tis wonder that enwraps me thus,
Yet 'tis not madness. Where's Antonio then?
I could not find him at the Elephant.
Yet there he was, and there I found this credit,
That he did range the town to see me out.
His counsel now might do me golden service:
For though my soul disputes well with my sense
That this may be some error, but no madness,
Yet doth this accident and flood of Fortune
So far exceed all instance, all discourse,
That I am ready to distrust mine eyes,
And wrangle with my reason that persuades me
To any other trust, but that I am mad,
Or else the Lady's mad; yet if 'twere so,
She could not sway her house, command her followers,
Take, and give back affairs and their dispatch,
With such a smooth, discreet, and stable bearing
As I perceive she does. There's something in't
That is deceivable. But here the Lady comes.

THE MURDER IN THE RED BARN

(This play is from an anonymous Victorian melodrama. The acting style should be melodramatic and over-acted. William Corder has murdered the beautiful Maria Marten and is now to be punished for his crime).

William Corder:

So ends my dream of wealth, tried, condemned today to be executed. Hundreds are flocking now to see me suspended between heaven and earth, the murderer's doom. Since my trial night after night, I have tried to sleep, but 'twas denied me. But now when sleep eternal rapidly approaches in the form of death my eyes grow weary, my eyelids close on the world of misery and thought.

(He falls asleep, and the ghost of Maria Marten appears too him).

Away, away, I dare not gaze upon that ghastly form - tis gone, a dream! How terrible! My brain reels, my flesh it quivers, and my heart it throbs to bursting.

Such undistinguished horrors make my brain
Like Hell the seat of darkness and of pain.

(Mr Marten, Maria's father enters to speak with Corder before he is condemned).

Mr Marten, I swear it is circumstantial evidence they have convicted me on. I am innocent, innocent.

Mister Marten, your words have touched my heart. I will confess to you what I denied to my judge. I am guilty. Yes, I did kill Maria, but I have known no rest from that moment. I have suffered a thousand years of agony. Nightly the murdered spirit of Maria appears before me calling down heaven's justice. But now, as I slept, I thought she came to me, not as I last saw her in death at my feet but in all her radiant beauty. It was our marriage day, the bells rang out, we entered the Church, and the words of the good priest were spoken. I was about to place the ring up on her hand when it fell from my grasp upon the marble pavement and shattered in a thousand pieces. I stopped to gather them. When the stones rolled back amidst a crash of thunder and there below, I saw horrid demons and loathsome serpents sporting fearfully midst burning flames. I looked at Maria, a change had come, the fair flesh had fallen from her body and there I saw a ghastly skeleton. Her eyes shot sparks of fire, her hands had changed to eagle's claws and seized my throat. She bore me down, down, yelling 'Welcome, murderer to thy future home!' Oh, torture horrible!

(Mr Marten asks Corder to repent).

Farewell, bless you for your forgiveness. Still from the scaffold I will proclaim – *(The ghost of Maria Marten appears again)* – Guilty!

THE RAILWAY CHILDREN
BY E. NESBIT

(Peter and his sisters have discovered an injured man in the railway tunnel and have taken him home to treat him and to call the doctor. Peter is fascinated by the blood and gore, unlike his two sisters who are a little squeamish).

Peter:

It *is* horrible, but it's very exciting. I wish doctors weren't so stuck up about who'll they'll have in the room when they're doing things. I should most awfully like to see a leg set. I believe the bones crunch like anything ... How are you going to be Red Cross Nurses, like you were talking of coming home, if you can't even stand hearing me say about bones crunching? You'd have to *hear* them crunch on the field of battle and be steeped in gore up to the elbows ... It would be a jolly good thing for you if I were to talk to you every day for half an hour about broken bones and people's insides, so as to get you used to it. I'll tell you what they do, they strap the broken man down so that he can't resist or interfere with their doctorish designs, and then someone holds his head, and someone holds his leg – the broken one, and pulls it till the bones fit in – with a crunch, mind you! Then they strap it up and – let's play at bone-setting! I'll get the splints and bandages; you get the couch of suffering ready.

Now then. (*He lies down and plays the agonised patient*). Not so tight. You'll break my other leg ... That's enough, I can't move at all. Oh, my poor leg! *(The two sisters run away leaving their brother Peter tied up).* You beasts! I'll yell, and Mother will come. I don't care if you never untie me, if that's your idea of a joke, Bobbie! You've made me feel pretty sick, I can tell you. (*Peter shakes off the loose cords and stands up*).

THE SNOWMAN
BY HANS CHRISTIAN ANDERSEN

(The snowman is talking to a yard-dog. Snowman is eager to experience what it is like in front of a warm fire).

Snowman:

It is so delightfully cold, that it makes my whole body crackle. This is just the kind of wind to blow life into one. How that great red thing up there they call the sun is staring at me! It shall not make me wink. I shall manage to keep the pieces.

There it comes again, from the other side. Ah, I have cured it of staring, though; now it may hang up there, and shine, that I may see myself. If I only knew how to manage to move away from this place. I should so like to move. If I could, I would slide along yonder on the ice, as I have seen the boys do; but I don't understand how; I don't even know how to run.

I don't understand you, yard-dog. Is that thing they call the sun up yonder to teach me to run? I saw it running itself a little while ago, and now it has come creeping up from the other side. What I also see yonder is the moon, and the one before it is the sun. It will come again to-morrow, and most likely teach me to run down into the ditch by the well; for I think the weather is going to change. I can feel such pricks and stabs in my left leg; I am sure there is going to be a change.

I don't understand it but I have a feeling that it is something very disagreeable. The sun is not my friend; I can feel that too. The cold is delightful.

Yard-dog, what is a stove? Does a stove look beautiful? Is it at all like me?

But there are people who are not men of snow, who

understand what it is. You lived in a house once. Why did you leave the stove? How could you give up such a comfortable place?

(The Snow Man looks into the house where the stove stands on its four iron legs, looking about the same size as the Snow Man himself.)

What a strange crackling I feel within me. Shall I ever get in there? It is an innocent wish, and innocent wishes are sure to be fulfilled. I must go in there and lean against it, even if I have to break the window.

What do you mean, yard-dog, if I approach the stove, I'll melt away. I might as well go in for I think I am breaking up as it is. All day I have stood looking in through the window, and in the twilight hour the room becomes still more inviting, for the stove gives a gentle glow, not like the sun or the moon; no, only the bright light which gleams from a stove when it has been well fed. When the door of the stove opens, the flames dart out of its mouth. How beautiful it looks when it stretches out its tongue?

Oh, I am so stove sick?

JANE EYRE
BY CHARLOTTE BRONTE

(John Reed is a schoolboy of fourteen years, large and stout for his age. He enjoys bullying his younger cousin, Jane Eyre).

John Reed:

Bah! Madam Mope! Where the dickens is she? Lizzy! Georgy! Georgiana! Jane is not here: tell Mamma she is run out into the rain – bad animal!

(Jane comes out from her hiding place, behind the curtain).

What do I want? Say, 'What do you want, Master Reed?' I want you to come here! This is for your impudence in answering mamma awhile since and for your sneaking way of getting behind curtains, and for the looks you had in your eyes two minutes since, you rat! What were you doing behind the curtain? Reading? Show the book. You have no business to take our books; you are a dependent, mamma says; you have no money; your father left you none; you ought to beg, and not to live here with gentlemen's clothes at our expense. Now, I'll teach you to rummage my bookshelves: for they are mine; all the house belongs to me or will do in a few years. Go and stand by the door, out of the way of the mirror and the windows. *(John hurls the book at Jane).* What? Wicked and cruel – slavedriver! Did she say that to me? Did you hear her, Eliza and Georgiana? Won't I tell mamma? But first – you rat! You rat – I'll show you! *(John drags Jane by the hair).*

THE LITTLE MERMAID
BY HANS CHRISTIAN ANDERSEN

(The prince meets the little mermaid for a second time and eventually realises it was she who had saved her life).

Prince:

Yes, you are dear to me for you have the best heart, and you are the most devoted to me; you are like a young maiden whom I once saw, but whom I shall never meet again. I was in a ship that was wrecked, and the waves cast me ashore near a holy temple, where several young maidens performed the service. The youngest of them found me on the shore and saved my life. I saw her but twice, and she is the only one in the world whom I could love; but you are like her, and you have almost driven her image out of my mind. She belongs to the holy temple, and my good fortune has sent you to me instead of her; and we will never part.

The maiden belongs to the holy temple, therefore she will never return to this world. And so, we will meet no more.

I must travel. I must see this beautiful princess; my parents desire it; but they will not oblige me to bring her home as my bride. I cannot love her; she is not like the beautiful maiden in the temple, whom you resemble. If I were forced to choose a bride, I would rather choose you, my dumb foundling, with those expressive eyes. *(He kisses her rosy mouth, plays with her long waving hair, and lays his head on her heart.)* You are not afraid of the sea, my dumb child, I will tell you of the storm and of the calm, of strange fishes in the deep beneath them, and of what the divers have seen there. *(He suddenly realises it is her).*

I see now that it was you, who saved my life when I lay dead on the beach. Oh, I am too happy, my fondest hopes are all fulfilled. You will rejoice at my happiness; for your devotion to me is great and sincere.

NOAH
BY ANDRE OBEY (1935)

(Noah is preparing the ark, whilst talking to God).

Noah:

Lord … Lord … Lord! Yes, Lord, it's me. Extremely sorry to both you again, but … What's that? Yes, I know, You've other things to think of, but after I've once shoved off, won't it be a little late? … Oh, no, lord, no, no, no … Of course, I trust You! You could tell me to set sail on a plank – a branch – on just a cabbage leaf … Yes, You could even tell me to put out to sea with nothing but my loincloth, even without my loincloth – completely – Yes, Lord, I beg your pardon, I know Your time is precious. Well, this is all I wanted to ask You. Should I make a rudder? Very good. Of course, winds, currents, tides …
storms! Oh, and while You're there just one other little thing … Are You listening, Lord?

Gone! He's in a bad temper … Well, you can't blame Him. He has so much to think of. All right; no rudder. No Lord, I'm not afraid. I know that You will be with me.

(He goes to the Ark). Storms! … I think I'll just put a few more nails in down here. *(He hammers and sings).*

When the boat goes well, all goes well.

When all goes well, the boat goes well.

And when I think that a year ago, I couldn't hammer a nail without hitting my thumb. That's pretty good, if I do say so myself. (*He climbs aboard the Ark and stands there like a captain).* Larboard and starboard! Cast off the hawsers! Close the portholes! Wait till the squall's over! … Now I'm ready, completely ready, absolutely ready! I'm ready. Well, I should like to know how all this business is going to begin. Magnificent weather – oppressively hot and no sign of a cloud. Well, that part of the programme is His look-out.

(He sees many animals boarding the Ark).

Another animal ... It's a zoo ... Sit down, monkey, sit down. Now, look here, my pets, here have I been working every day for a whole year and not one of you has ever shown me the tip of his nose before. Are you out to make trouble for me now that I've finished my work?

Good morning, old fellow. Now, if I understand you rightly, you want to come on board, eh? Stop! I didn't say you could! ... Well. All right. I'll let you come aboard. No, I don't see anything against it. So, the time has come! All right. Up with you!

Lord, what marvels there are on the threshold of this new life. It will take a stout heart, a steady hand, and a clear eye! Ah, well, if You've chosen me, perhaps it's because I am the least wicked of the herd. Come, all aboard. Make yourselves at home! Straight ahead, across the deck! Down the stairway to the left. You'll find your cabins ready. They may look like cages, but they'll be open always. Hurry, you lazybones, you slow-coaches, creepy crawlers; you who travel in herds and you who walk alone – Hurry! Everyone! Get aboard!

THE SILVER CHAIR
BY C.S. LEWIS

(This is from the 6th book of the Chronicles of Narnia. Eustace and Jill have freed the gnomes and cut off the Witch's head. Golg asks Eustace and Jill if they would like to stay at the bottom of the world with the gnomes rather than return home).

Golg:

Your Honours, your Honours, why don't you come down to Bism? You'd be happier there than in that cold, unprotected, naked country out on top. Or at least come down for a short visit. We do not live or swim in the fire-river itself. Not we. It's only salamanders live in the fire itself. It is hard to tell their kind, your Honour, for they are too white-hot to look at. But they are most like small dragons. They speak to us out of the fire. They are wonderfully clever with their tongues: very witty and eloquent. Down there, I could show you real gold, real silver, real diamonds. I have heard of those little scratches in the crust that you Topdwellers call mines. But that's where you get dead gold, dead silver, dead gems. Down in Bism we have them alive and growing. There, I'll pick you bunches of rubies that you can eat and squeeze you a cup full of diamond-juice. You won't care much about fingering the cold, dead treasures of your shallow mines after you have tasted the live ones of Bism.

If your Honours are really set to go back to overworld, there is one bit of the road that's rather lower than this. And perhaps, if that flood's still rising –

But there are lamps all the way. Your Honour can see the beginning of the road on the far side of the chasm. Goodbye to Your Honours, I'm off!

THE SILVER CHAIR
BY C.S LEWIS

(This is from the 6th book of The Chronicles of Narnia. Eustace Scrubb is talking to Jill Pole. They are at school and Jill has been crying as she has been bullied).

<u>Eustace:</u>

A lot of queer things happened to me in the hols. Look here, Jill Pole, you and I hate this place about as much as anybody can hate anything, don't we? I really think I can trust you. I say, are you good at believing things? I mean things that everyone here would laugh at? Could you believe me if I said I'd been right out of the world – outside this world – last hols? Supposing I told you I'd been in a place where animals can talk and where there are – enchantments and dragons – and – well, all the sorts of things you have in fairy-tales. I got there – by Magic. I was with two cousins of mine. We were just – whisked away. They'd been there before. When we came back from That Place, someone said that the two Pevensie kids (that's my two cousins) could never go there again. It was their third time, you see. I suppose they've had their share. But he never said I couldn't. Surely, he would have said so, unless he meant that I was to get back? And I can't help wondering, can we – could we? Let's draw a circle on the ground – and write in queer letters in it - and stand inside it – and recite charms and spells. I've never done it. I'm not sure that he'd like it. It would look as if we thought we could make him do things. But really, we can only ask him. Aslan. They call him Aslan in That Place. It can't do any harm, just asking. Let's stand side by side, like this. And we'll hold out our arms in front of us with the palms down: like they did in Ramnadu's island. Oh, I'll tell you about that another time. And he might like us to face the east. Let's see, where is the east? It's an extraordinary thing about girls that they never know the points of the compass. That's the east, facing up into the laurels. Now, will you say the words after me? Aslan, Aslan, Aslan!

THE HORSE & HIS BOY
BY C.S. LEWIS

(Shasta meets a talking horse).

Horse:

Hush! Not so loud. Of course, I can talk. Where I come from, nearly all the animals talk. I come from Narnia. The happy land of Narnia – Narnia of the heathery mountains and the thymy downs, Narnia of the many rivers, the plashing glens, the mossy caverns and the deep forests ringing with the hammers of the Dwarfs. Oh, the sweet air of Narnia! An hour's life there is better than a thousand years in Calormen. *(He whinnys like a sigh).* I was kidnapped, or stolen, or captured – whichever you like to call it. I was only a foal at the time. My mother warned me not to range the Southern slopes, into Archenland and beyond, but I wouldn't heed her. And by the Lion's Mane, I have paid for my folly. All these years I have been a slave to humans, hiding my true nature and pretending to be dumb and witless like *their* horses.

I didn't tell them I was here because I am not such a fool, that's why. If they'd found out I could talk they would have made a show of me at fairs and guarded me more carefully than ever. My last chance of escape would have been gone. We mustn't waste time on idle questions. You want to know about my master the Tarkaan Anradin. Well, he's bad. Not too bad to me, for a war horse costs too much to be treated very badly. But you'd better be lying dead tonight than go to be a human slave in his house tomorrow. You had better run away. Run away with me. I will run away too if you'll come with me. This is the chance for both of us. You see, if I run away without a rider, everyone who sees me will say "Stray horse" and be after me as quick as he can. With a rider I've a chance to get through. That's where you can help me. On the other hand, you can't get very far on those two silly legs of yours (what absurd legs humans have!) without being overtaken. But on me you can outdistance any other horse in this country. That's where I can help you. By the way, I suppose you know how to ride?

You've ridden a donkey! In other words, you *can't* ride. That's a drawback. I'll have to teach you as we go along. If you can't ride, can you fall? Can you fall and get up again without crying and mount again and fall again and yet not be afraid of falling? We'll make a fine rider of you in time. And now – we mustn't start until those two in the hut are asleep. Meantime we can make our plans.

AUTHOR INDEX

Peter Pan by J.M. Barrie (1911)

The Wizard of Oz by L. Frank Baum (1900)

Alice in Wonderland by Lewis Carroll (1865)

The Pied Piper of Hamelin b Robert Browning (1842)

Aladdin (an ancient folktale)

Hansel & Gretel by the Grimm brothers 1812)

The Princess & the Swineherd by Hans Christian Anderson (1841)

King Midas (8th Century)

The Chronicles of Narnia (1950)

The Magician's Nephew by C.S. Lewis

The Lion, the Witch & the Wardrobe by C.S. Lewis

The Voyage of the Dawn Treader by C.S. Lewis

The Horse & his Boy by C. S. Lewis

Great Expectations by Charles Dickens (1860)

Hard Times by Charles Dickens (1854)

Oliver by Charles Dickens (1838)

A Christmas Carol by Charles Dickens (1843)

The Secret Garden by Frances Hodgson Burnett (1911)

The Snow Queen by Hans Christian Anderson (1844)

Puss in Boots by Perrault (1697)

The Tinder Box by Hans Christian Anderson (1835)

Worzel Gummidge by Barbara Euphan Todd (1936)

Toad of Toad Hall by Kenneth Grahame (1929)

The House at Pooh Corner by A.A. Milne (1928)

Tom Sawyer by Mark Twain (1876)

Pinocchio by Carlo Collodi (1883)

The Happy Prince by Oscar Wilde (1888)

The Remarkable Rocket (1888) by Oscar Wilde (1888)

Androcles & the Lion by George Bernard Shaw (1915)

Heidi by Johanna Spiri (1880)

A Midsummer Night's Dream by William Shakespeare (1600)

Henry V by William Shakespeare (1600)

King John by William Shakespeare (1623)

The Merchant of Venice by William Shakespeare (1600)

Twelfth Night by William Shakespeare (1602)

The Murder in the Red Barn (unknown Victorian)

Noah by Andre Obey (1934)

The Railway Children by E. Nesbit (1906)

The Snowman by Hans Christian Andersen (1861)

The Little Mermaid by Hans Christian Andersen (1837)

ABOUT THE AUTHOR

Kim Gilbert trained as a professional actress at the Guildford School of Acting, studied for an LGSM with the Guildhall School of Music and Drama and took an English degree at the Open University. She has been acting, teaching and directing plays and musical productions for more than 35 years. She has experience in a wide range of theatre, TV and voiceover work. She has a First-class Honours degree in English and has taught English and Drama in many top schools in the country. Kim has examined for Lamda for a number of years and has also acted as an adjudicator. She has been running Dramatic Arts Studio for 15yrs, a private drama studio which specialises in developing excellence in all forms of performance and communication.

OTHER BOOKS BY THE SAME AUTHOR:

<u>Shakespeare Scenes</u>
Monologues for young adult female actors
Monologues for young female actors
Duologues for female actors
Duologues for male actors
Monologues for young male actors
Monologues for young teen actors
Duologues for male/female actors

<u>Chekhov Scenes</u>
Monologues & Duologues for women
Monologues for Male Actors
Duologues from Anton Chekhov

<u>Scenes from Oscar Wilde</u>
Monologues & Duologues for female actors
Monologues for Male actors
Duologues from Oscar Wilde

Classic Monologues for female actors
Classic Monologues for male actors
Classic Duologues for female actors
Classic Acting Monologues for Girls (8-14yrs)
Duologues for girls & boys aged 8-14yrs
Acting Duologues for boys & girls aged 5-10
<u>Monologues & duologues from the Greeks</u>
<u>Duologues for male & female actors from the works of Charles Dickens</u>
<u>Restoration Drama</u>
Monologues for male & female actors
Duologues for male & female actors

<u>Improve Your Voice</u>
How to speak English with confidence

Available from Amazon Bookstore

Thank you for reading! If you enjoyed this book or found it useful, I would be grateful if you'd post a short review on Amazon. Your support really does make a difference and I read all the reviews personally so I can get your feedback and make this book even better.

Printed in Great Britain
by Amazon